Country Mailboxes

Patterns & Techniques

Patrick Spielman
& Paul Meisel

 Sterling Publishing Co., Inc. New York

A special thanks to Arthur E. Meisel for getting me started in woodworking many years ago. There could be no better friend, teacher, confidant, and—above all—father.

Paul Meisel, 1992

Library of Congress Cataloging-in-Publication Data

Spielman, Patrick E.
    Country mailboxes / by Patrick Spielman and Paul Meisel.
        p.   cm.
    Includes bibliographical references and index.
    ISBN 0-8069-8673-5
    1. Woodwork—Amateurs'   manuals.   2. Mailboxes—Amateurs' manuals.   I. Meisel, Paul, 1946–   .   II. Title.
TT185.S643   1993
684.1′8—dc20   92-41648
                                                             CIP

10   9   8   7   6   5

Published by Sterling Publishing Company, Inc.
387 Park Avenue South, New York, N.Y. 10016
© 1993 by Patrick Spielman and A. Paul Meisel
Distributed in Canada by Sterling Publishing
% Canadian Manda Group, P.O. Box 920, Station U
Toronto, Ontario, Canada M8Z 5P9
Distributed in Great Britain and Europe by Cassell PLC
Villiers House, 41/47 Strand, London WC2N 5JE, England
Distributed in Australia by Capricorn Link Ltd.
P.O. Box 665, Lane Cove, NSW 2066
Manufactured in the United States of America

Sterling ISBN 0-8069-8673-5

Metric Equivalents

INCHES TO MILLIMETRES AND CENTIMETRES

MM—millimetres   CM—centimetres

Inches	MM	CM	Inches	CM	Inches	CM
⅛	3	0.3	9	22.9	30	76.2
¼	6	0.6	10	25.4	31	78.7
⅜	10	1.0	11	27.9	32	81.3
½	13	1.3	12	30.5	33	83.8
⅝	16	1.6	13	33.0	34	86.4
¾	19	1.9	14	35.6	35	88.9
⅞	22	2.2	15	38.1	36	91.4
1	25	2.5	16	40.6	37	94.0
1¼	32	3.2	17	43.2	38	96.5
1½	38	3.8	18	45.7	39	99.1
1¾	44	4.4	19	48.3	40	101.6
2	51	5.1	20	50.8	41	104.1
2½	64	6.4	21	53.3	42	106.7
3	76	7.6	22	55.9	43	109.2
3½	89	8.9	23	58.4	44	111.8
4	102	10.2	24	61.0	45	114.3
4½	114	11.4	25	63.5	46	116.8
5	127	12.7	26	66.0	47	119.4
6	152	15.2	27	68.6	48	121.9
7	178	17.8	28	71.1	49	124.5
8	203	20.3	29	73.7	50	127.0

Table of Contents

Color section follows page 32.

Introduction

The rural mailbox has been around for over 100 years. As we drive along the roadside, we see many mailboxes in advanced stages of deterioration. Some actually appear to have been around since rural mail delivery was first approved by United States postmaster John Wanamaker in the 1890s.

In recent years, manufacturers have offered such design innovations as moulded plastic barns and the like. These mass-produced mailboxes are not especially interesting or unusual. Every now and then, we've all seen a homemade mailbox that could be labelled "roadside art." These rare visual treats delight the rural traveller. Today, the trend to decorate and beautify the old, mundane mailbox is growing. After all, the mailbox is your property; it identifies your home; and it's the first visual impression for visitors, guests, and passersby.

This book will assist craftspeople who want to lay claim to a unique local landmark—the mailbox. This book provides designs and ideas for distinctive mailboxes that reflect the interests or professions of their owners.

Country Mailboxes provides over 20 plans in almost as many different designs, to permit you to transform a typical mailbox into something special. The plans include vehicles, animals, buildings, and even a western saddle and a boy fishing.

Each design is accompanied by all the necessary drawings, a list of materials, instructions, and painting suggestions. Thus, it is easy to create mailboxes that are identical to those shown in the full-color section, which follows page 32. Since certain construction techniques are the same for every mailbox, this information appears in Chapter 1, "Basic Techniques." On the same note, because many of the vehicle mailboxes involve similar construction procedures, that information is presented in Chapter 8, "Four Fun Vehicles."

i-1. This condition is typical of many mailboxes along our country roadsides. These are all good candidates for replacement.

4

i-2. Mailboxes converted to unique vehicles. Notice how the round top of the mailbox is the perfect hood for these vehicles.

Neither elaborate home workshops nor expensive tools are required to build the projects in this book. Most homeowners already have the basic tools, and most materials are available locally. We have even included optional plans and suggestions for making drum and disc sanders, for those who wish to become more involved in the fascinating and rewarding hobby of woodworking.

Every design in this book is the work and effort of Paul Meisel and his staff at Meisel Hardware Specialties, P.O. Box 70, Mound, MN 55364. Before selecting the projects for this book, we created design sketches for over 100 different mailbox concepts. We then developed what we felt were a representative assortment of plans to appeal to many homeowners.

Incidentally, as a matter of convenience for the reader, full-size patterns of every design in this book—as well as for a number of other mailbox designs and some special hardware, such as vehicle

i-3. Paul Meisel with one of his most advanced and challenging creations. Note: Because of space limitations, the plans for this carousel-horse mailbox are not included in this book. Plans, instructions, and special hardware may be purchased from Meisel Hardware Specialties, P.O. Box 70, Mound, MN 55364.

wheels—are available from Paul's company.

Together, Paul and I have prepared this volume of his copyrighted designs for use by the homeowner/woodworker. Wherever space allows, we have included full-size patterns of parts. Some patterns will require enlargement by the reader.

It is obvious that making and selling mailboxes using the designs in this book has outstanding commercial potential for the enterprising craftsperson. Permission is hereby granted to individuals or companies to make up to 200 pieces per design without restriction. Merchandising quantities beyond that, either assembled or in kit form, would dilute the market and requires the written permission of Paul Meisel. Understandably, large-quantity production would lessen the uniqueness of the works created by individuals using this book. This would be in direct conflict with our primary purpose, which is to help in the creation of something special and uncommon.

Patrick Spielman

1
Basic Techniques

The mailbox designs in this book involve cutting wood shapes and fastening them to a standard metal mailbox. Because methods of cutting and finishing are similar for each project, this chapter provides the basic techniques common to all the projects in this book. You may want to select your project design first and then refer back to this chapter before actually beginning to build.

Each project in this book was designed with postal regulations (see Appendix) in mind. We believe they conform to all postal requirements. We checked with our local postmaster, and he could find no reason why any of these projects would not be acceptable to other postmasters or mail carriers across the country.

Purchasing Metal Mailboxes

Even if your existing metal mailbox is in relatively good condition, consider purchasing a new one, to enhance the overall look of the finished project.

Most projects in this book ask for a prepainted metal mailbox with a baked-on factory finish, which will save you time and effort. Mailboxes are inexpensive and readily available.

Most projects in this book use the standard-size mailbox known as T1 or 1. Depending on the manufacturer, these mailboxes may be made from smooth or ribbed metal. They are available in aluminum, steel, or plastic. Steel mailboxes are either prepainted or made of galvanized steel. For the projects in this book, smooth-metal, manufacturer-prepainted mailboxes are preferred.

The "Domestic Mail Manual," published by the United States Postal Service, lists the manufacturers of traditional and contemporary mailboxes that have been approved by the Postal Service. The 1992 manual also gives guidelines for the three standard sizes of traditional mailboxes. This manual refers to the small, medium, and large mailboxes as T1, T2, and T3, respectively. This is a

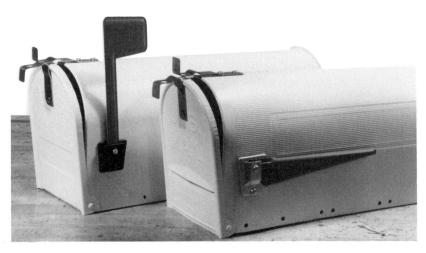

1-1. Prepainted mailboxes are used for most of the projects in this book. The mailbox on the right has a ribbed finish and a small door slot. Either smooth or ribbed mailboxes work well for the projects in this book. The authors prefer mailboxes without mail slots in the doors.

1-2. Some solid woods suitable for mailbox components. Left to right: clear redwood, No. 2 pine, clear poplar.

change from the 1991 manual, which refers to the same small, medium, and large mailboxes as size 1, 1A, and 2, respectively. Expect to see both numbering systems.

Wood Materials

You will need good wood materials, but they need not be expensive. Economical solid woods and sheet materials are available locally. The projects in this book are made from pine or fir and exterior-grade plywood. Both hold up well outdoors, as long as they are properly finished.

Solid Woods. No. 2 pine and utility-grade woods often have knots and defects. With careful layout, you can cut around these defects, leaving them in the waste area. As a rule, choose soft woods, such as pine, fir, or redwood. Avoid fresh-cut lumber and pressure-treated woods. When they are cut, pressure-treated woods produce dangerous sawdust and fumes that are better avoided. Clear pine and redwood are expensive but easy to work. All solid woods are available in standard, ¾" thickness. Construction-grade fir is available in 1½" thickness in the form of 2 × 4 and 2 × 6 boards.

Panel and Sheet Materials. Exterior-grade A/C fir plywood is the most practical choice. It is available in thicknesses of ¼", ⅜", ½", and ¾". The primary disadvantage is that it often has an irregular surface and numerous voids in the interior plies. Also, it may have some edge voids that need filling in. Fir plywood has a rough surface that requires a

fair amount of priming and sanding to get a smooth surface for painting.

Another good choice of sheet material is sign painters' plywood. Sold under various brand names, including Duraply and Medex, this material has very smooth surfaces. Duraply has a resin-impregnated craft-paper overlay that is applied to one or both surfaces. Sign makers' plywood has few interior voids, if any. Speak with your local building-materials supplier; or, since the designs in this book require relatively small pieces, check with your local sign painters to see if they have any small scraps they can give you or sell very inexpensively.

Another excellent material is Finnish birch plywood. Like sign painters' plywood, it is weather-resistant, virtually void-free, and extremely smooth on both sides. Another major advantage is it is available in a large variety of thicknesses. If you have trouble finding it locally, order it from mail-order catalogs. Be sure any plywood you choose is rated for use outdoors.

1-3. Exterior-quality sheet materials include, left to right: Finnish birch, fir plywood, and two different types of sign painters' plywood—medium-density overlay (MDO) and Duraply brand sheet stock with resin-impregnated paper bonded to each surface.

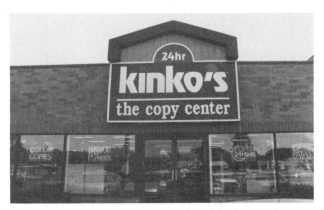

1-4. The easiest way to enlarge drawings is with the help of a photocopy machine. Visit your local library, printer, or copy shop.

Enlarging and Transferring Patterns

Most designs in this book have been reduced to fit the page size and save space. Some smaller parts are given as full-size patterns, and they are so noted. Here are two ways to enlarge designs to make your own full-size patterns.

Photocopiers. The most convenient way to enlarge patterns from this book is with a photocopier. Many photocopiers are capable of enlarging up to 200% in one-percent increments. Many local libraries have enlarging copiers for public use. Or, to locate a company that specializes in photocopying, check the Yellow Pages of your phone book under the heading "Photocopying."

Enlargement by Squares. All the irregular-shaped profiles and designs in this book that require enlarging were drawn with a grid of squares. Craftspeople have been using the square-grid technique for decades to enlarge designs and create full-size patterns. The usual procedure is to draw the required number of squares (of the size specified on the drawing) onto a large piece of paper. Next, using the squares as a guide, copy the design freehand on the grid, square by square. Draw the curves by eye, after plotting their direction with reference to the surrounding square(s). Graph paper is available preprinted with 1″ squares. If you are drawing grid lines to make your own graph, you may wish to lay out 2″ grid patterns to save time. Of course, you must skip every other line in the grid pattern provided in this book.

Once you have the enlarged pattern roughly drawn, smooth out the curves and use a straightedge to make the straight lines crisp.

Transferring Patterns to the Wood. Full-size patterns can be transferred to wood in several ways. Some people prefer to scissor-cut the pattern to a rough size and attach it directly to the wood. This can be done using rubber cement or special spray adhesives, as shown in 1-5. Spray a very light mist to the back of the paper pattern only. Do *not* spray directly onto the wood. Test the spray beforehand with a small piece of paper and a small wood sample, to ensure that the pattern adheres sufficiently for cutting, yet peels off easily afterwards.

Patterns can also be transferred by scissor-cutting them to their final shape and carefully tracing them with a sharp pencil.

Some craftspeople prefer the traditional method of carbon or graphite transfer paper, shown in 1-6.

Tip: It is a good idea to mark in advance the location of the holes that will need to be drilled. The

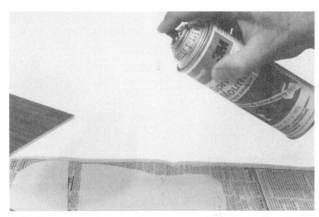

1-5. One type of aerosol temporary-bonding adhesive is 3M® Scotch Spray Mount Artist's Adhesive #6065. Note that the pattern is scissor-cut to a rough size and a newspaper catches the overspray.

1-6. Transferring the pattern using carbon paper.

1-7. Use a scratch awl to mark the location of all holes.

1-9. Sawing with a scroll saw.

easiest way is to mark through the pattern with a scratch awl. See 1-7.

Sawing. Straight-line cutting can be accomplished with hand saws, hand-held power saws, or machines such as band saws and table saws. The latter produce the best straight-line cuts, but a table saw is not a necessity. Hand-held electric sabre saws are satisfactory for most sawing jobs. Clamp the work so the cutting is done beyond the edge of your workbench or sawhorse. See 1-8.

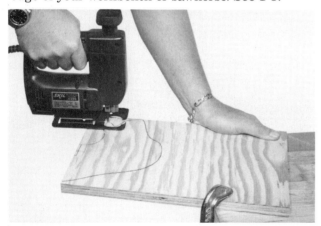

1-8. Sawing an irregular curve with a hand-held sabre saw.

Scroll saws (1-9) and band saws (1-10) are best for making accurate, curved cuts. When using a scroll saw, always select a blade appropriate for the thickness of material. With a band saw, a ⅛" blade is good for cutting patterns that have tight curves.

Edge-Sanding and Smoothing. These are typically performed after sawing and again just prior to finishing. Sometimes, sawed edges need to be sanded to improve or "fair" the overall profile shape

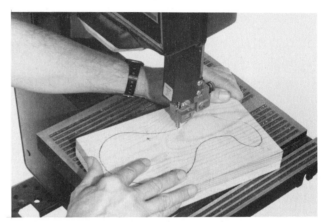

1-10. Cutting mailbox parts with a band saw.

of the part. Other times, sanding is necessary to smooth the sawed edge and remove saw marks. Most sanding can be accomplished with drum and disc sanders. Use a drum sander for all inside curves and a disc sander for outside curves and straight lines. Drum sanding can be done on a drill press or on a commercial or homemade drum sander.

The sanding drums shown in 1-11 accept regular, flat-sheet abrasives rather than the more expensive preformed sleeves. Sanding drums are available in various diameters, to accommodate different sizes of inside curves.

Tip: The abrasive paper used on a sanding belt from a belt sander can be cut and the pieces then used to load these drums. The rugged cloth backing will make these sheets last much longer than ordinary paper-backed sheet sandpaper.

Making a Drum Sander (1-12). This can be accomplished easily by using a salvaged motor held vertically in a simple, wood, boxlike structure that

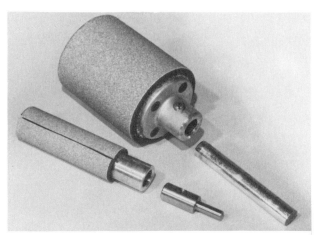

1-11. Sanding drums are available in various sizes. The auxiliary ½″ straight shaft and the ½″ to ¼″ reduction shaft pictured allow this type of drum to be used in a drill press with a ¼″ or ½″ chuck capacity. These drums will also mount directly to the ½″ motor shaft of the shop-made drum sander.

1-13. Sanding a sawed edge of an inside curve to its final shape. Note that the drum's entire abrasive surface can be utilized by holding the project off the work table and moving the edge of the stock "freehand" from left to right.

1-12. This shop-made drum sander utilizes a salvaged ¼ H.P. motor.

1-14. Another timesaving technique is to hold the piece at a 45-degree angle and lightly soften the sharp arris (the place where the edge and face of the wood meet).

also functions as the work table. All that is required is a ¼ H.P. washing machine or furnace motor. Simply bolt it inside the box with its shaft in the vertical position. Sanding drums like those in 1-11 mount directly to the motor shaft with a single set screw. This allows the drum size to be changed quickly.

The specifications for making a shop drum sander are given in 1-15 and 1-16 and in the List of Materials (Table 1-1).

General Construction Procedure. The height of the sides and support blocks and the size and location of the dadoes and holes will vary according to the size of the motor. Some motors may require custom-made mounting brackets. These instructions are for a motor measuring 4¼″ from base to center. Adjust the dimensions accordingly. This motor has a metal motor mount that attached easily to the plywood side. Some motors may require improvised mounting brackets.

After determining the sizes needed to fit the motor, lay out the parts and cut them. Cut a ⅛ × ¼″ dado in the sides. Cut a 3⅛″ diameter hole in the top and a ⅝″ diameter hole through the dust shield. Attach the sides to the top and bottom with wood screws and glue. Assemble the motor mounts, if necessary, and mount the motor and dust shield.

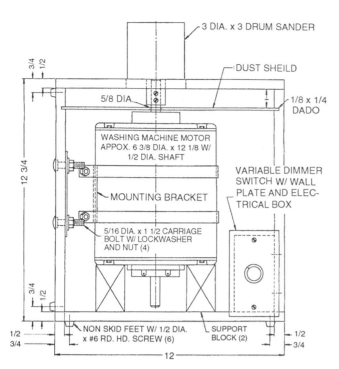

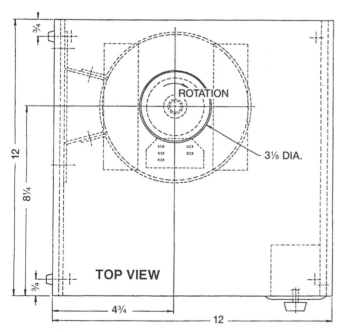

1-15. Side-view details of the shop-made drum sander. Note that the dimmer switch shown may not work on all motors.

TOP VIEW

NOTE: NON-SKID FEET ARE MOUNTED ON BOTH BOTTOM AND SIDE OF HOUSING TO ALLOW THE MACHINE TO BE USED IN EITHER THE VERTICAL OR HORIZONTAL POSITION.

1-16. Top-view details of the shop-made drum sander. The motor is mounted towards the back, to provide a larger work surface in the front.

Table 1-1—List of Materials		
Quantity	Part	Size of Material
1	Top	$\frac{1}{2} \times 12 \times 12$
1	Bottom	$\frac{1}{2} \times 12 \times 12$
2	Sides	$\frac{1}{2} \times 11\frac{3}{4} \times 12$
1	Dust shield	$\frac{1}{8} \times 11\frac{1}{2} \times 12$
1	Motor	110 Volt, $\frac{1}{2}$" dia. shaft
1	Wall or dimmer switch w/wall plate & box	
4	Carriage bolts with lock washers & nuts	$\frac{5}{16}$ dia. $\times 1\frac{1}{2}$
2	Support blocks	$1\frac{1}{2} \times 2\frac{1}{2} \times 5\frac{1}{2}$
1	Motor mount	
8	Non-skid feet	$\frac{1}{2}$ dia. $\times \frac{1}{4}$
1	Sanding drum w/sleeve	

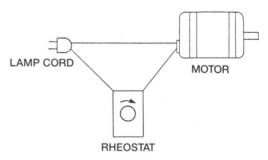

1-17. A general wiring diagram. Be sure the motor and switch are properly grounded and that any moving parts are safely guarded.

Important: Make sure the motor shaft is perpendicular to the top. Attach the non-skid feet and electrical box. Wire the motor. See 1-17.

Making a Disc Sander. A simple plywood disc with abrasive glued to it can be mounted to the table or radial-arm saw arbor or in the wood lathe as an accessory. Although not intended for heavy cutting or continuous work, this tool is ideal for light sanding of convex curves and straight lines (1-18). The disc is just a piece of flat plywood. The abrasive is glued to it with temporary bond-type spray. The disc is mounted to an inexpensive arbor. Like the inexpensive drill stand, it is available at most hardware stores. Shim the drill slightly in the drill stand or at the base, if necessary, to make the surface of the abrasive disc run at 90 degrees to the table. See 1-19.

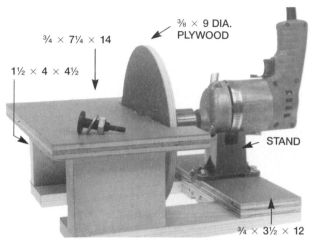

1-18. This shop-made, electric-drill-driven disc sander will smooth outside (convex) curves quickly and easily. An arbor (as shown on the table) and a plastic drill-stand clamp (optional) are purchased components.

1-19. Using a disc sander to sand the outside curve of a dalmatian mailbox leg.

Building a Typical Mailbox

Making the Baseboard. Begin each project by cutting the baseboard. Rural mailboxes are recessed at the bottom. Place a ¾″ piece of plywood or solid stock underneath the mailbox in this recess. This baseboard will make it easier to mount the mailbox to the post. It will also anchor many of the wood parts to the side of the mailbox.

Since the baseboard is concealed from view as well as from the weather, it makes little difference what type of material is used. Exterior plywood, ¾″ pine, and fir all work well. The baseboard should fit snugly in the recess under the mailbox. The baseboard should be approximately 1″ shorter in length than the mailbox. It should butt against the back and leave clearance in the front for the door. See 1-20.

1-20. The baseboard fills the recess in the bottom of the mailbox. Note that it is shorter than the mailbox, allowing clearance for the door operation.

Attach the baseboard temporarily to the underside of the mailbox with two or more sheet metal screws. See 1-21 and 1-22. Rural mailboxes have holes prepunched along the lower edge of the sides and back. Install screws through these holes. It may be necessary to remove the baseboard for some steps of procedure, depending on the nature of the design. You may want to remove the baseboard to mount the completed mailbox to the post.

Tip: Mark the baseboard so you will know which way it is installed, since you may have to remove it. If it is installed backwards or upside down, the holes will not line up.

Building a Shop Stand. Working on a mailbox can be awkward because of the size and shape it develops as components are fastened to it.

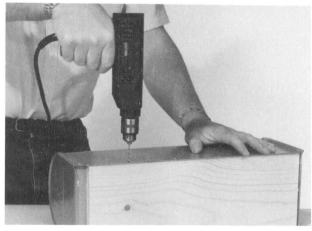

1-21. Installing a baseboard on a #1 size rural mailbox. This mailbox requires a 6⅛ × 17½″ base. Drill ⁷⁄₆₄″ pilot holes through the prepunched holes and into the wood.

1-22. Attach the baseboard temporarily, using one or two sheet metal screws in each side.

Making a simple stand gets the mailbox off the workbench and positions it at a comfortable working height. This makes it much easier to attach parts, especially those that hang below the bottom of the mailbox, such as animal legs or vehicle wheels.

A simple stand can be made using a 4 × 4 post about 48″ long. Cut four support feet from scrap plywood or solid stock and attach them to the bottom of the post for stability. See 1-23 and 1-24.

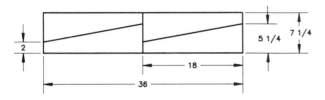

1-23. Layout details for making the four support feet for the shop stand.

1-24. This simple shop stand makes working on the mailbox easier. Drill holes 1½″ from the wide end of each support and assemble with wood screws.

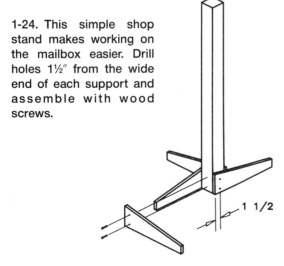

An alternative idea to a floor stand is simply to clamp a shorter-length 4 × 4 vertically into the workbench vise or to clamp it to the side of the bench itself.

Remove the baseboard from the mailbox and attach it to the stand with long screws, as shown in 1-25. Finally, reattach the mailbox and secure it with at least two sheet metal screws. See 1-26.

1-25. The baseboard is attached directly to the end of the 4 × 4″ shop stand. Secure it with 3″ screws or with angle brackets.

Fastening Mailbox Decorations with Screws. Two basic types of screws are used: (1) sheet metal screws, and (2) drywall screws. See 1-27.

Sheet metal screws are available in several head shapes, including pan and hex head. Use hex-head sheet metal screws for fastening from the inside of the mailbox.

Drywall screws are available with regular flat heads or smaller trim heads (or "finishing heads"). Trim-head screws can be drawn flush with the surface of the wood without having to be countersunk.

14

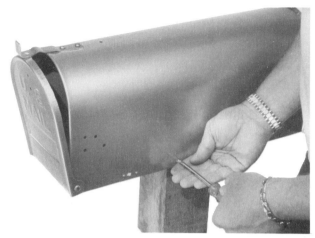

1-26. Temporarily reattach the mailbox to the baseboard.

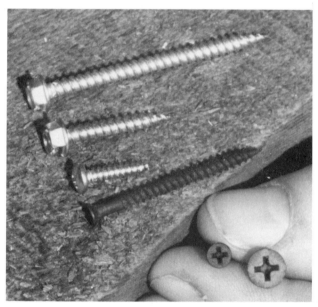

1-27. Hex-head sheet metal screws, shown in the upper portion of the photo, can be fastened with a socket wrench. The wrench simplifies the task of installing screws from the inside of the mailbox. Drywall screws, shown at the bottom, are available in both regular-head and trim-head styles. A trim-head screw, like a finishing nail, is less conspicuous.

After all the parts have been cut and sanded, position them on the mailbox and drill the screw holes. Attach the pieces with screws so they can be removed later for painting. The position of the individual pieces will determine whether the screws are installed from the outside or the inside of the mailbox.

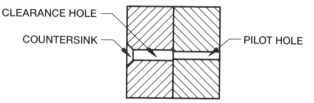

1-28. The clearance hole is the same diameter as the shank of the screw. Pilot holes are smaller, so the screw threads can grab and hold. The funnel-shaped hole is made with a countersink. Trim-head screws have very small heads and can be driven flush from the surface without countersinking.

Two hole sizes are necessary to secure the screws. The **clearance hole** is drilled through the top piece of wood. It is approximately the same size as the outside dimension of the shank of the screw so the screw can just slide through the hole. The **pilot hole** is smaller and holds the screw threads. See 1-28.

All the projects in this book specify either #6 or #8 screws. For #6 screws, use a $\frac{9}{64}''$ diameter clearance hole and a $\frac{7}{64}''$ diameter pilot hole. For #8 screws, use an $\frac{11}{64}''$ diameter clearance hole and a $\frac{1}{8}''$ diameter pilot hole.

Installing Trim-Head Finishing Screws from Outside the Mailbox. Wood decorations positioned near the bottom of the mailbox are easiest to install by driving screws through the decoration, through the bottom lip of the mailbox, and into the wood baseboard. Trim-head finishing screws are easier and quicker to install than regular, flat-head screws because they require no countersinking. The small head allows them to be driven with a screwdriver until the head is flush with the surface of the wood. See 1-29–1-33 to learn how to attach a dalmatian-project leg using $2\frac{1}{4}'' \times$ #6 trim-head finishing screws.

A screwdriver is better than a screw gun for installing trim-head finishing screws, because it is easier to control the exact depth of the screw. Tighten the screw until the screw head is just flush with the surface of the plywood.

Tip: The heads of these finishing screws strip rather easily, so be sure to use a good-quality #1-size Phillips screwdriver with a good tip. Even if the pilot holes are predrilled into the baseboard, it is important to push down hard with the screwdriver to prevent the Phillips screw slots from rounding out. By driving the trim-head finishing screws until the heads are flush with the surface of

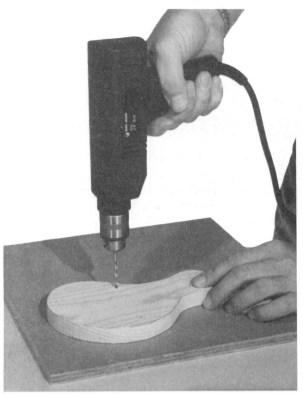

1-29. Step 1: Drill clearance holes all the way through the wood decoration with a %₆₄" diameter drill.

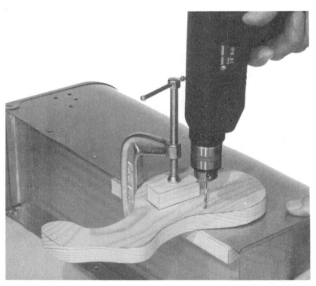

1-30. Step 2: With the baseboard removed, position the rear leg. A piece of scrap wood protects the leg from being marked by the C-clamp. Another piece of scrap is placed behind the lip of the mailbox to support the sheet metal as it is drilled. Using the %₆₄" clearance holes in the leg as a drilling guide, drill holes through the metal lip of the mailbox.

1-31. Step 3: After all the legs have been drilled, replace the baseboard and drill ⅞₆₄" pilot holes for the #6 finishing head drywall screws.

1-32. Step 4: Use a #1 Phillips screwdriver to install #6 trim-head finishing screws. Tighten just until the heads are flush with the surface of the stock.

the wood, it will not be necessary to fill or plug the holes. Use this mounting method on all decorations that are secured directly to the baseboard with the screws driven from the outside of the mailbox inward.

Wood parts that mount close to the front of the mailbox must not get in the way of the flag. A ½" wood spacer must be used to allow clearance for flag operation. See 1-33 and 1-34.

Installing Sheet Metal Screws from Inside the Mailbox. This technique is used to secure parts to the outside surface of the mailbox. Sheet metal screws with hex heads are best for this. The procedure is shown in 1-35—1-42.

1-33. Installing the front leg is similar to the rear-leg procedure, shown in 1-29, except a small, ½″ thick plywood spacer block must be placed between the front leg and the mailbox to allow clearance for the mailbox flag.

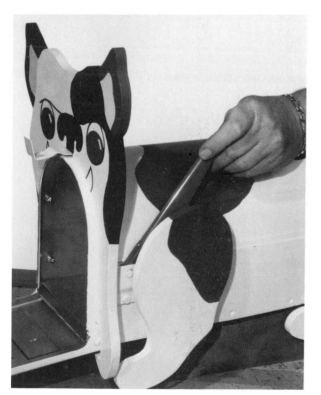

1-34. Installing ½″ thick spacers behind the parts that attach near the front of the mailbox allows room for the flag to operate freely.

Begin by positioning the piece on the mailbox. In the case of the dalmatian, first center the head on top of the mailbox. Position it just far enough forward so the back of the notch in the head just touches the back tip of the mailbox latch.

Once the wood piece has been positioned properly, tilt it up slightly and mark the location of the holes with a felt-tip pen. Before doing so, consider the length of the screw, and be sure the hole is not so close to the back of the neck that the screw comes through. For the dalmatian, it was possible to remove one screw from the latch and use that hole for one attachment screw. See 1-35.

Gently centerpunch the surface of the metal mailbox to help start the drill bit, then drill the hole. See 1-36–1-37. Reposition the part and use a pencil or scratch awl to mark the location for the pilot holes. See 1-38. Remove the decoration and drill ⅛″ pilot holes in the wood piece. See 1-39.

It may be awkward to fit a screwdriver inside the mailbox. Simplify the job by using hex-head sheet metal screws, and then substitute a socket wrench for a screwdriver. See 1-42.

Note: On some drawings, such as the mouth of the fish and the tails on the horse trailer, the suggested location of the pilot hole is marked.

Interior Anchor Cleats. When installing larger, vertically mounted decorations such as the dalmatian head, a curved cleat positioned inside the mailbox will add a great deal of support and strength to the project. See the cutting diagram, 1-40. The upper radius of this support should be the same as the inside radius of the mailbox. To lay out this curve, measure the inside width of the mailbox, then open a compass to an amount equal to one-half the width of the mailbox. For example, if the inside width of the mailbox measures 6¼″, set the compass to 3⅛″, and swing an arc on a piece of scrap plywood. Next, reduce the compass setting by ¾″, to create the smaller radius of the cleat. The cleat should be approximately 4″ long and made from ¾″ thick stock.

After cutting the cleat, drill the ¹¹⁄₆₄″ clearance hole (1-41). Sand a small, flat spot (approximately ¾″ wide) on top of the cleat to help ensure a tight fit when the screws are tightened. The thin metal on the top of the mailbox will flatten out when sandwiched between the cleat and the piece that is attached.

Illus. 1-42 shows how two curved cleats support the dalmatian's head. Use 2″ × #8 sheet metal

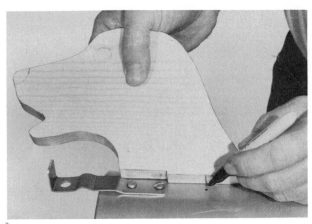

1-35. Step 1: To attach components to the surface of the mailbox with screws driven from the inside of the mailbox in an outward direction, first mark the location of the screw holes to be drilled in the mailbox. Mark the location with a permanent-ink felt-tip pen.

1-37. Step 3: Drill 11/64″ clearance holes through the mailbox for a #8 sheet metal screw.

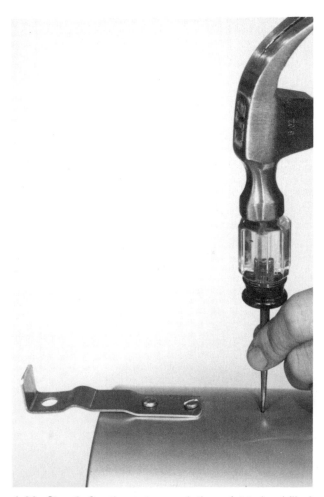

1-36. Step 2: Gently centerpunch the point to be drilled, to prevent drill bit wander.

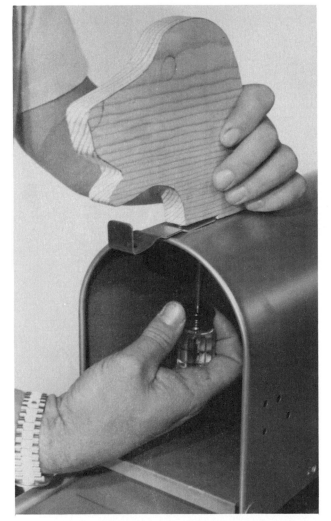

1-38. Step 4: Reposition the decoration and mark the location of the pilot holes with a scratch awl.

1-39. Step 5: Drill ⅛″ pilot holes.

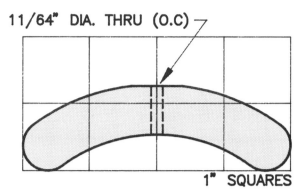

11/64″ DIA. THRU (O.C)

1″ SQUARES

1-40. Step 6: Typical layout for a curved cleat for a size #1 rural mailbox. Note the flat space on top of the cleat. The top curve should equal the inside radius of the metal box.

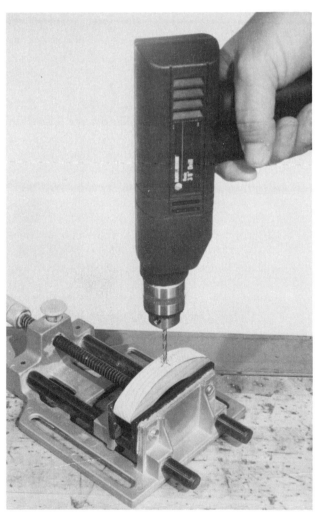

1-41. Step 7: Drill a ¹¹⁄₆₄″ diameter clearance hole through the center of the cleat for a #8 sheet metal screw.

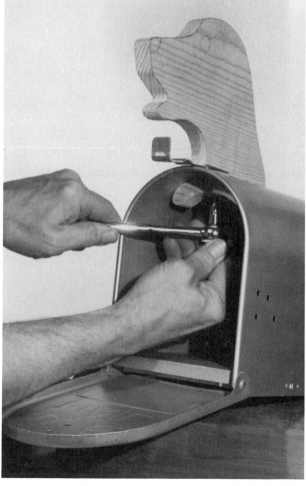

1-42. Step 8: Sheet metal screws are installed with a socket wrench. Two screws and two cleats firmly attach the dog's head to the mailbox.

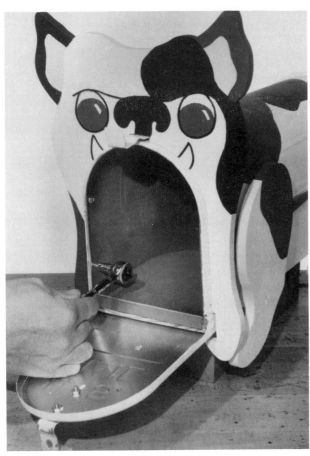

1-43. Vertical decorations that go across the axis of the mailbox do not require an inside wood cleat support. Use #8 hex-head sheet metal screws to install this type of decoration.

screws. The screws go through the cleat, through the holes in the top of the mailbox, and into the pilot holes in the wood head.

Some exterior parts do not require interior support cleats. Designs like the bulldog's head follow the curve of the mailbox and provide their own supporting strength. See 1-43.

Adhesives. Some wood parts are glued together either for added strength or to simplify assembly. Select a glue rated for exterior use, such as Weldwood® Plastic Resin Glue and Titebond® II Wood Glue. See 1-44.

Finishing. Distinctively different painting techniques are used for the wood parts and for the metal mailbox. The following suggestions explain how to prepare and paint both types of surfaces. All painting should be saved for last. It is best done with all the pieces removed from the mailbox.

1-44. Choose a glue rated for exterior use, such as Weldwood® Plastic Resin or Titebond® II waterproof glue.

Preparing Wood Surfaces. Standard fir plywood is notorious for having voids on the interior veneers. It is good to fill these voids after all stock is cut and rough-sanded. Use a wood filler rated for outdoor use. Also, fill knots and other blemishes on the surface of the plywood. See 1-45 and 1-46.

After sanding, brush on one or two coats of primer.

Tip: Paint primers with an alcohol or shellac base are especially good for sealing knotty wood. In 1-47, the wood parts for the dalmatian are covered with two coats of Bin Primer Sealer. Because this primer dries very rapidly, fairly heavy coats were applied. This gives a smooth finish even to plywood that has minor surface blemishes. A final coat of latex- or oil-based exterior paint should be applied over the primer. A foam brush works well.

Spray Painting. Using standard spray equipment is an option you may want to consider. It is ideal for applying single-color primers and base coats. Aerosol sprays can also be used, but this is a more expensive method of application.

Paint Markers. Use a black paint marker to fine-line details and outline certain features. These are similar to felt-tipped markers, except that they contain paint, which is much more durable than ink. Like felt-tipped pens, paint markers are easy to use for continuous thin lines, such as the outlines on the duck head. See 1-49.

1-45. Fill voids with wood putty. Choose a product rated for exterior use. The surface of this piece of sheathing is exceptionally rough and would require not only that the knot holes be filled, but that the entire surface be covered as well.

1-46. Sanding the plywood surface with a sanding block.

1-47. Prepare the wood with two coats of good-quality white primer.

1-48. Paint pens are useful for painting thin lines, such as for facial features. Unlike felt-tip pens, they contain real paint.

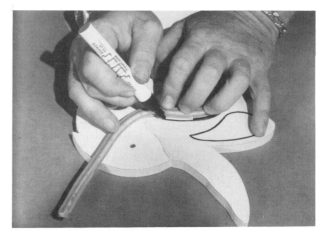

1-49. Using a black paint pen to apply accent lines. Paint pens can be used freehand or with a flexible curve.

Prepainted Mailboxes. Factory prepainted rural mailboxes (rather than galvanized ones) are preferred for the projects in this book. Most manufacturers provide them in a variety of colors. Purchasing a prepainted mailbox will eliminate additional painting on certain projects. For example, the duck requires a white mailbox and the locomotive a black one. Some projects, however, such as the fish or the tri-wing airplane, begin with a white mailbox but require additional painting.

Certain precautions should be observed when painting on the shiny surface of a prepainted mailbox. To ensure that the paint adheres, wipe on a liquid surface preparation, such as Imperial Wil-Bond.® This no-sanding deglosser will help guarantee a tight bond with either solvent- or latex-based paints. **Caution:** Deglossers, as the name implies, change a glossy finish to a flat finish. Use them only on areas to be painted. In 1-50–1-51 a prepainted silver mailbox has been deglossed and painted white. On some projects, such as the goose, where only a portion of the finish is to be painted over, either degloss just the area to be painted or—instead of deglossing—use a solvent-based enamel you have tested and know will adhere. No deglosser was used on the dalmatian mailbox shown in 1-52.

An alternative method of deglossing is to rough up the surface of the area to be painted with 220-grit sandpaper.

It is important to prepare the surface of the mailbox so paint will adhere. Test the paint on a small area, to be sure it is compatible and adheres well. Let the sample area dry for 48 hours, and test for adhesion with a piece of masking tape.

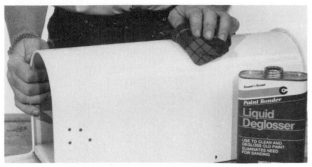

1-50. For prepainted mailboxes, wipe on a deglosser, to help guarantee that the paint adheres.

1-51. A solvent-based aerosol enamel gives a smooth finish when applied over a factory-prepainted white mailbox. On mailboxes such as the goose, airplane, and fish, where only a portion of the mailbox is painted, use masking tape to cover the areas not being painted.

1-52. For adding brushed-on details to mailboxes, solvent-based enamel is best.

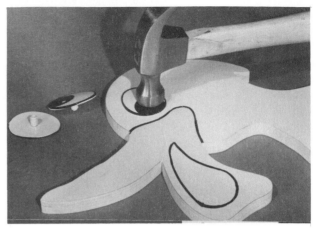

1-53. Plastic eyes with shanks eliminate tricky detail painting. Tap the eyes into the hole with a hammer.

For metal mailboxes, solvent-based enamel in aerosol spray cans provides a smooth, glossy finish. See 1-51.

Painting Galvanized Mailboxes. Because it is difficult to get paint to adhere to galvanized surfaces, special care must be taken in selecting a good primer. Most hardware stores carry a primer suitable for galvanized rain gutters and downspouts. These primers work also on galvanized mailboxes. Once primed, these mailboxes can be painted with a brush or an aerosol spray.

Plastic Animal Eyes. These are moulded from one piece of plastic and have a solid shank. They are easily installed by drilling a hole in the wood equal to the diameter of the shank. Plastic eyes eliminate a difficult painting job. See 1-53.

Mounting Your Mailbox. Either a steel pipe and floor flange or a 4 × 4 post can be used to mount your mailbox (1-54). For multiple mailboxes, a piece of 2 × 6 or 2 × 8 construction fir supported by 4 × 4 posts works well. You will have to vary the construction slightly to allow for mailbox designs with decorations that hang below the mailbox, such as duck feet or vehicle wheels.

City dwellers and those who are not required to locate their box on the roadway can still make and use any of the designs in this book. One method of attaching the mailbox to the side of the house appears in 1-54.

Before installing your mailbox be sure to read the postal regulations in the Appendix, pages 154–155. It is also a good idea to check with your mail carrier to determine the preferred height.

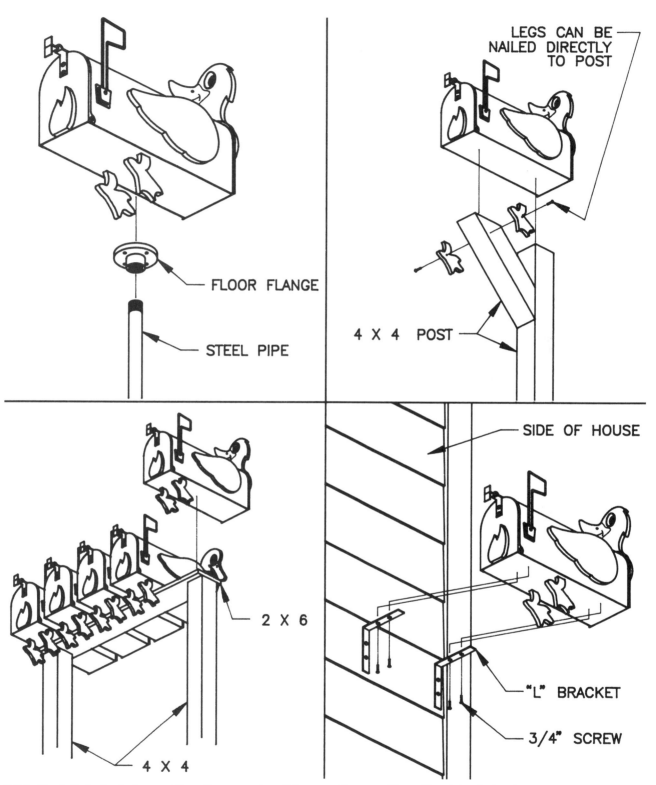

LEGS CAN BE NAILED DIRECTLY TO POST

FLOOR FLANGE

STEEL PIPE

4 X 4 POST

SIDE OF HOUSE

2 X 6

4 X 4

"L" BRACKET

3/4" SCREW

1-54. *Top left:* A steel pipe and floor flange work well for mounting a mailbox. *Top right:* A simple 4 × 4″ wood post can be fashioned to hold a mailbox, or purchase ready-made mounting posts at hardware stores or do-it-yourself centers. *Bottom left:* This simple rack holds multiple mailboxes. *Bottom right:* Urban homeowners can mount a rural mailbox to the side of their home.

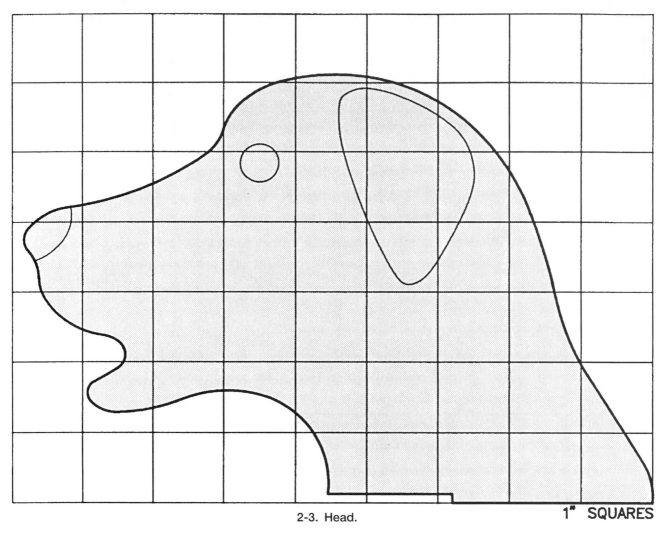

2-3. Head.

1″ SQUARES

tail. Attach the tail with two 1″ × #8 sheet metal screws.

Finishing

Sanding. Remove all wood pieces from the mailbox and finish sanding. Fill any voids with wood putty.

Ears. Glue an ear to each side of the head, as shown in 2-3.

Painting. Use white and black paint for the dalmatian. (Or paint to resemble any breed of dog you wish.) Prime and paint all wood parts white. A factory-painted white mailbox simplifies the job. General painting tips are given on page 22.

To make the black spots, we used a ¾″ flat glaze brush and made short strokes, so the spots are not

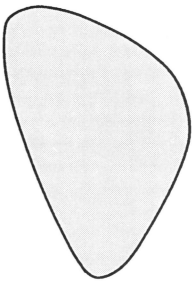

2-4. Ear, full-size pattern.

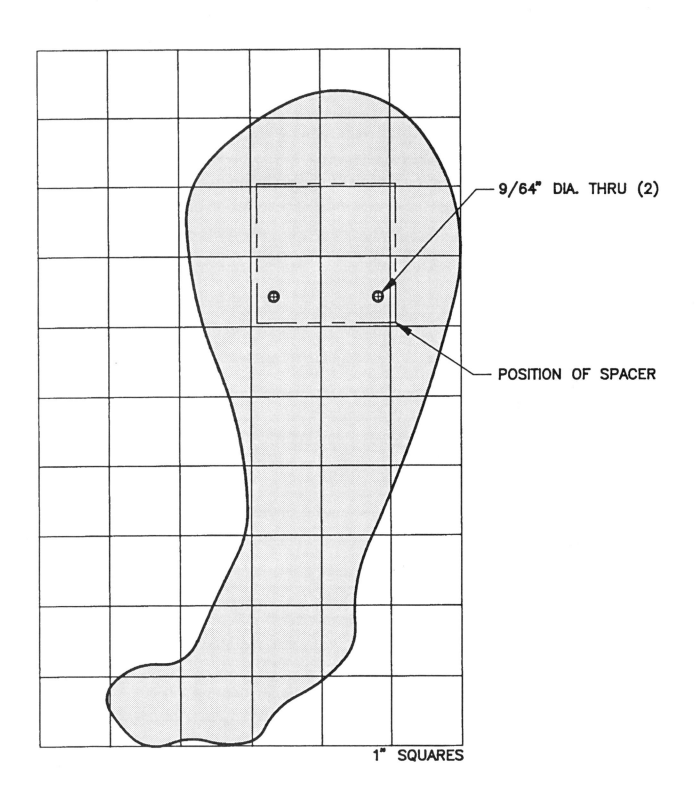

9/64" DIA. THRU (2)

POSITION OF SPACER

1" SQUARES

2-5. Front leg.

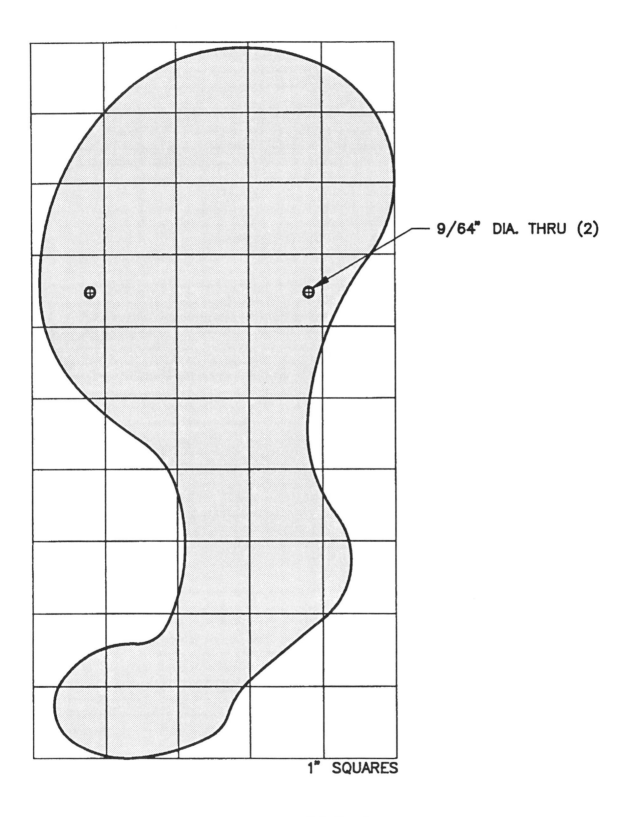

9/64" DIA. THRU (2)

1" SQUARES

2-6. Rear leg.

round but more or less rectangular. The location of the black spots is not critical. Simply "freehand" them, spacing them somewhat evenly around the mailbox.

The ears can be spotted or painted solid black. The eyes may be painted; or use plastic animal eyes.

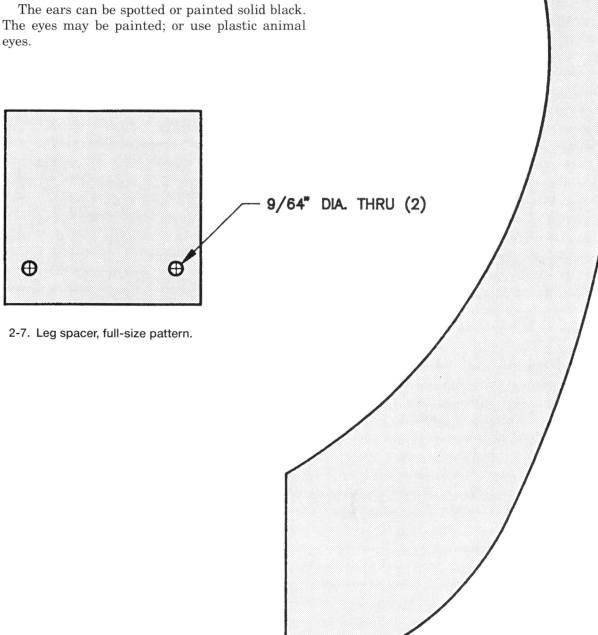

9/64" DIA. THRU (2)

2-7. Leg spacer, full-size pattern.

2-8. Tail, full-size pattern.

3

Bulldog

Every mail carrier we've talked with has had at least one story about an unnerving encounter with a dog. However, they all smile the first time they open this friendly bulldog mailbox.

This design accents the wide, flat face of the bulldog and its stout body shape. See the exploded assembly drawing, 3-2. Painting the details is relatively simple.

Table 3-1 lists all materials required.

Cutting the Parts

Baseboard. Cut out the baseboard and attach it temporarily to the mailbox with one screw on each side. (Additional screws will be added later when the legs are attached.)

Head. Enlarge the head pattern (3-3) to full size. Before transferring the pattern to the plywood, open the mailbox door and place the mailbox against the enlarged pattern, to be sure the pattern conforms exactly to the size and shape of the mailbox. Trace around the opening of the mailbox to ensure a perfect fit.

Transfer the head pattern to $\frac{1}{2}$″ thick stock and cut out. The notches on the pattern allow clearance for the door hinge.

After sanding, locate and drill the mounting holes. Position the head around the front of the box and as far forward as possible. Be sure the head does not interfere with the opening and the closing of the door. Attach the head to the mailbox with sheet metal screws installed from inside the mailbox. We used four sheet metal screws, evenly spaced around the head. Size #8 sheet metal screws require drilling $\frac{11}{64}$″ diameter clearance

holes in the mailbox and $\frac{1}{8}$″ diameter pilot holes in the plywood head. See Chapter 1, 1-34, page 17.

Legs. Enlarge the patterns for the front and rear legs (3-4–3-5). Transfer the patterns and cut a left and right piece for each set of legs. Another method is to stack-cut the legs. Nail two pieces of plywood together and cut both at the same time. See Chapter 8, 8-13, page 69.

Spacer. The purpose of the square spacer (3-6) is to keep the dog's left front leg slightly away from the mailbox, to give ample clearance for the mailbox flag. For symmetry, use a spacer next to the right front leg as well.

Attach the front legs about 1″ from the head. Mount the rear legs about 1″ from the back of the mailbox. Drill the holes for mounting the legs $\frac{3}{8}$″ from the bottom edge of the mailbox, so the mounting screws line up with the center of the baseboard edge.

The holes in the legs are designed so the screws can be driven through the legs, the leg spacers (where required), the bottom lip of the mailbox, and into the baseboard. We used $2\frac{1}{4}$″ × #6 trim-head screws, which require a $\frac{9}{64}$″ clearance hole and $\frac{7}{64}$″ pilot hole.

Tail. Attach the tail (3-7) to the back of the mailbox. The top of the tail should be located about 1″ down from the top of the mailbox back. Drill $\frac{11}{64}$″ diameter clearance holes in the back of the mailbox. With the tail held in position, reach into the mailbox and use a pencil to mark the location for the pilot holes in the tail. Drill the pilot holes with a $\frac{1}{8}$″ drill and attach the tail with two $\frac{1}{2}$″ × #8 sheet metal screws.

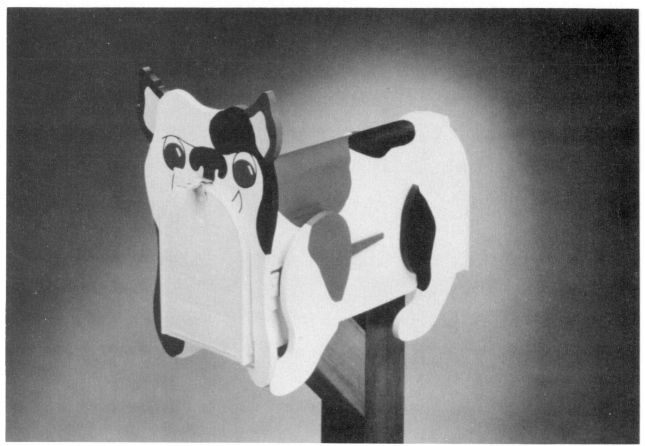

3-1. This design accentuates the broad face and stout body typical of all bulldogs.

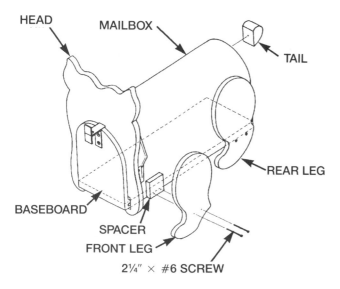

3-2. Exploded assembly drawing for the bulldog mailbox.

Table 3-1—List of Materials
(Dimensions are for a #1 or T1 rural mailbox)

Quantity	Part	Size of Material
1	Baseboard	*¾ × 6⅛ × 17½
1	Head	½ × 9⅞ × 15½
2	Front leg	½ × 5¾ × 9½
2	Rear leg	½ × 5⅞ × 10¼
2	Spacer	½ × 2 × 2
1	Tail	1½ × 1½ × 2⅛
8	Trim-head drywall screw	2¼ × #6
6	Sheet metal screw	½ × #8
1	Mailbox	Size #1 or T1

Exterior enamel paint recommended colors: white, black, brown, pink.

*Size of baseboard may vary, depending on the brand of mailbox.

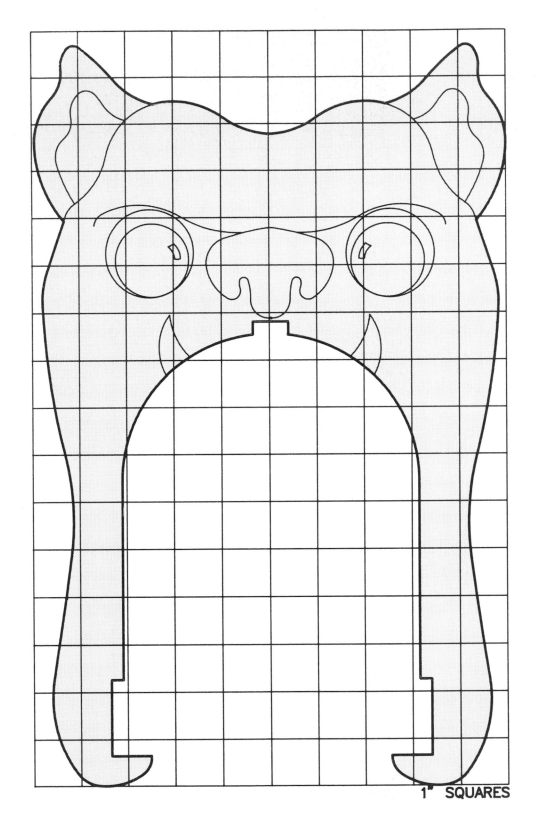

1" SQUARES

3-3. Head details.

Dalmatian

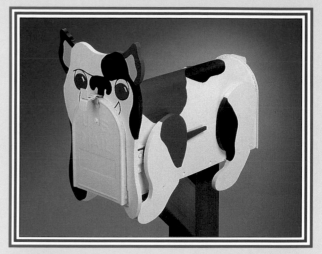

Bulldog

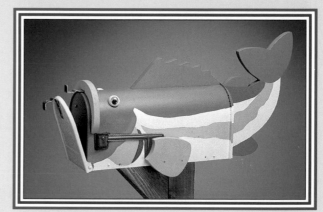

Largemouth bass

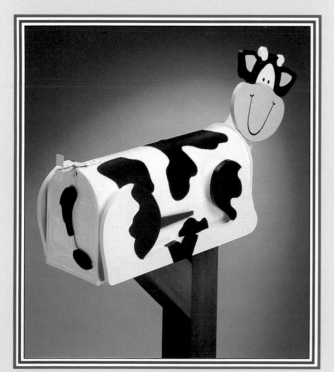

Cow

Canada goose

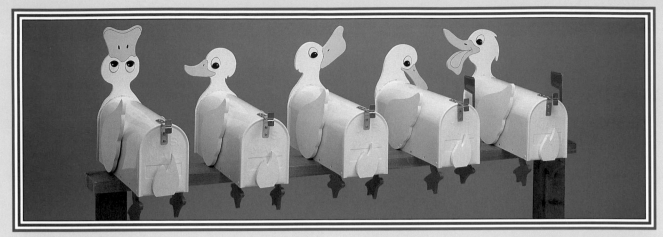

Ducks in a row

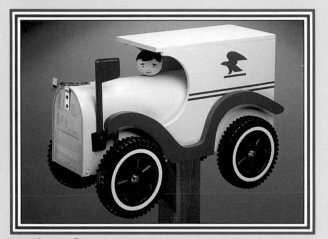

Mail truck

Pickup truck

Fire truck

Car with rumble seat

B

Tractor

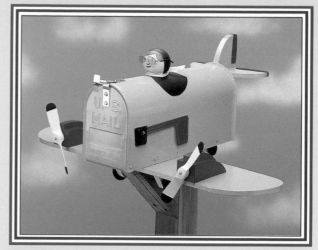

Single-wing airplane

Barn

Locomotive

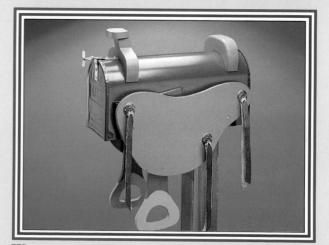

Western saddle

Horse trailer

Church

Tri-wing airplane

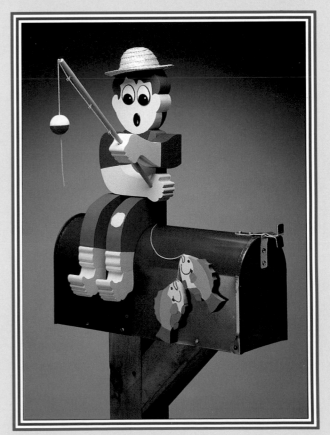

Fishing boy

D

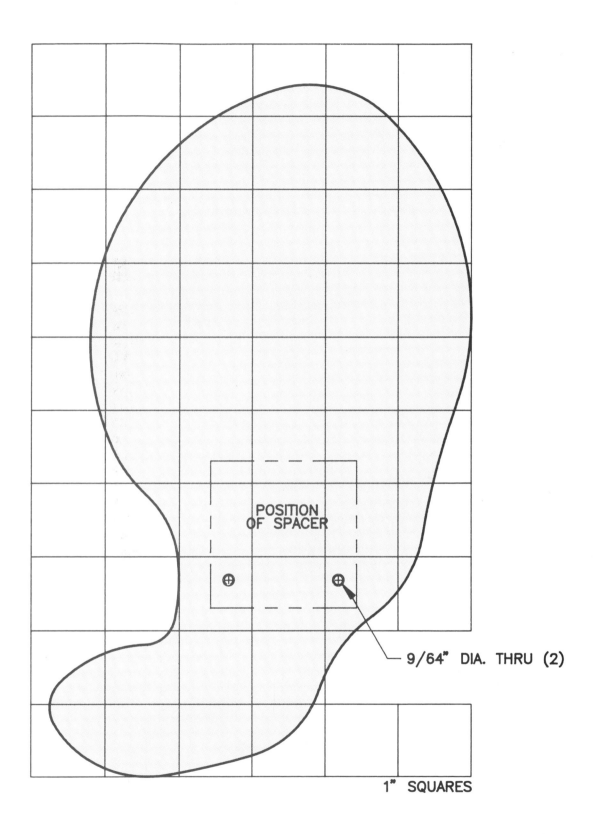

POSITION
OF SPACER

9/64" DIA. THRU (2)

1" SQUARES

3-4. Front leg detail.

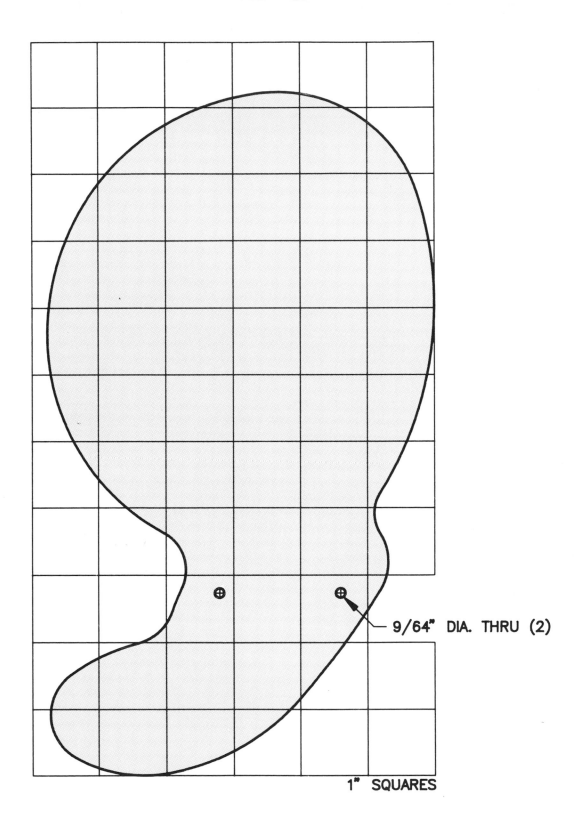

9/64" DIA. THRU (2)

1" SQUARES

3-5. Rear leg detail.

Finishing

Sanding. Remove all wood pieces and finish-sand. Fill any voids with wood putty.

Painting. We used white, light brown (or tan), black, and pink paint. Starting with a white mailbox simplifies painting. Outline the eyes and teeth with black paint. See 3-3. Use carbon or transfer paper to lay out the face details on the face piece. The location of the brown and black spots on the legs and mailbox itself is not critical. These spots can be "free-handed," as ours are, or—if you are extremely particular—try to duplicate the color scheme of your favorite bulldog. See Chapter 1 for additional tips on painting.

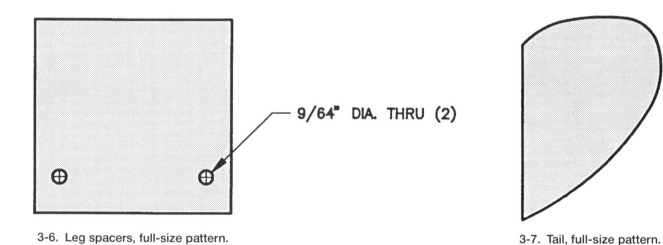

3-6. Leg spacers, full-size pattern.

9/64" DIA. THRU (2)

3-7. Tail, full-size pattern.

4

Cow

The black-and-white Holstein cow has become a popular motif in American "country" decorating.

This mailbox design features a Holstein with an extra-large head. The head is attached to the back of the mailbox, so it does not interfere with the operation of the door, but is clearly seen by passersby. The unique "sitting" position allows this mailbox and others to be supported on a common flat surface. See the exploded assembly drawing, 4-2.

Cutting the Parts

Baseboard. Cut out a baseboard to fit the mailbox, but do not install it.

Head, Muzzle, Legs, Spacers, and Tail. Cut these parts from $\frac{1}{2}$″ plywood. Enlarge the designs as necessary. See the drawings, 4-3–4-8.

Transfer the patterns to stock. Be sure to flip the leg patterns over to make left and right sides. Make four spacers. Smooth all sawed edges.

Neck. The neck piece (4-5) is cut from $1\frac{1}{2}$″ thick stock to provide solid support for the head. Cut this part from a piece of 2×6″ stock.

Drilling Holes and Attaching Parts

Head, Muzzle, and Neck. Attach the muzzle and head to the neck with a $2\frac{1}{4}$″ × #6 screw. Mark the location of the screw clearance holes (see 4-3–4-4), and drill through each piece with a $\frac{9}{64}$″ drill.

Drill a $\frac{7}{64}$″ pilot hole $1\frac{1}{4}$″ deep into the neck piece. See 4-5.

Before attaching the head and muzzle pieces to the neck, drill the mounting holes through the back of the mailbox to mount the neck.

The neck is approximately $\frac{1}{2}$″ from the top of the mailbox and is centered on the back end. Using the marking procedure described on page 18, mark two holes in the back of the mailbox with a pencil or felt-tip pen. Lightly centerpunch the holes and drill them with an $\frac{11}{64}$″ drill.

Reposition the neck, reach through the mailbox, and mark the location of the pilot holes to be drilled in the neck. Drill $\frac{1}{8}$″ pilot holes approximately 1″ deep. This is the correct hole size to attach the neck with size #8 sheet metal screws.

The head, muzzle, and neck can now be attached to the mailbox.

Legs and Spacers. Place the mailbox on its side, flag-side up. The baseboard should not be in position at this time. Place the leg spacers and legs on the side of the mailbox, with the leg spacers approximately 1″ from each end of the mailbox. Position the front of each leg piece so it is even with the front of the mailbox and aligned with the bottom of it. Make sure the flag operates without restriction.

With the legs and the spacers clamped in position, drill $\frac{9}{64}$″ diameter clearance holes through the legs, leg spacers, and bottom lip of the mailbox.

Before removing the clamps, mark each spacer for orientation; *i.e.*, flag side front, flag side rear, etc.

Place the baseboard under the mailbox and drill $\frac{7}{64}$″ pilot holes into the baseboard. Attach the legs and leg spacers with $2\frac{1}{4}$″ × #6 screws.

Tail. The tail is attached to the door of the mailbox with two $\frac{1}{2}$″ × #8 sheet metal screws. Position the tail on the door of the mailbox (4-1). Mark the location for two $\frac{11}{64}$″ clearance holes to be drilled in the door. Lightly centerpunch before drilling, to prevent drill-bit wander.

4-1. This sitting Holstein mailbox is definitely one of the best choices for authentic American country decorating.

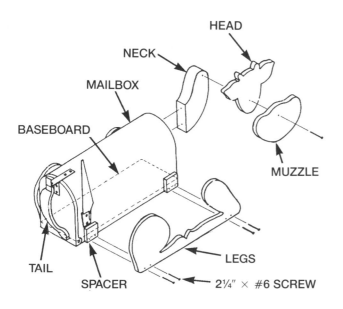

HEAD

NECK

MAILBOX

HEAD

BASEBOARD

MUZZLE

TAIL

LEGS

SPACER

2¼″ × #6 SCREW

4-2. Exploded assembly drawing.

Table 4-1—List of Materials
(Dimensions are for a #1 or T1 rural mailbox)

Quantity	Part	Size of Material
1	Baseboard	*¾ × 6⅛ × 17½
1	Head	½ × 7¼ × 9½
1	Muzzle	½ × 5½ × 7⅞
1	Tail	½ × 3 × 7⅛
2	Leg	½ × 7⅞ × 19⅛
4	Spacer	½ × 2 × 2
1	Neck	1½ × 4¼ × 8⅛
9	Trim-head drywall screw	2¼ × #6
2	Sheet metal screw	1 × #8
2	Sheet metal screw	½ × #8
1	Mailbox	Size #1 or T1

Exterior enamel paint recommendations: white, black, pink.

*Size of baseboard may vary, depending on the brand of mailbox.

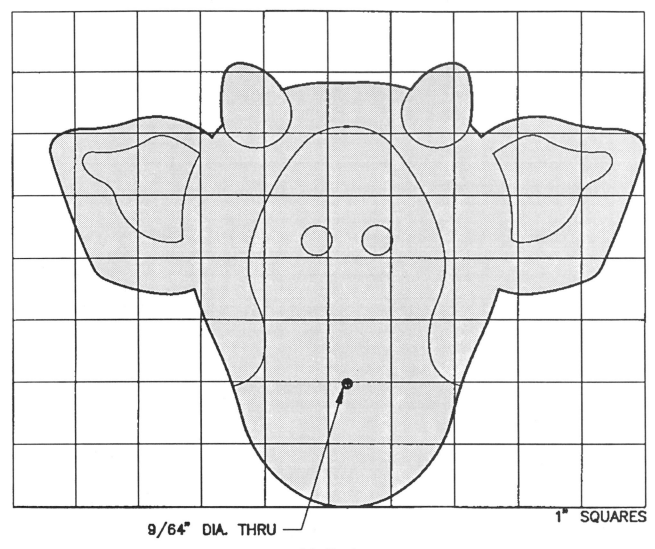

9/64" DIA. THRU —

1" SQUARES

4-3. Head.

Reposition the tail, and mark through the holes in the door to locate the pilot holes. Drill ⅛″ holes, approximately ⁷⁄₁₆″ deep, into the tail piece. To prevent the ½″ screws from breaking through the tail, place a small, flat washer under the head of each sheet metal screw.

Finishing

Wood Pieces. Disassemble all pieces for painting. Fill any voids in the plywood edges and finish-sand all pieces. Apply primer and white paint to all wood pieces.

Use carbon or graphite paper to transfer the design. Do this for the hooves on the leg pieces, the mouth on the muzzle piece, and the various details on the head piece. The location of the black spots on the wood pieces can be duplicated as shown in the drawings, or you can create your own style. Paint the cow white and apply black spots randomly. Paint the muzzle pink. Painting black spots on the edges of the leg parts will provide a nice contrast to the white mailbox background. Also, paint the hooves black. See 4-7.

Mailbox. A prepainted white mailbox will simplify painting. Refer to Chapter 1 for information about painting metal mailboxes.

Final Assembly

Reattach all pieces to the mailbox with screws. Touch up the screw heads with paint, so that they blend in.

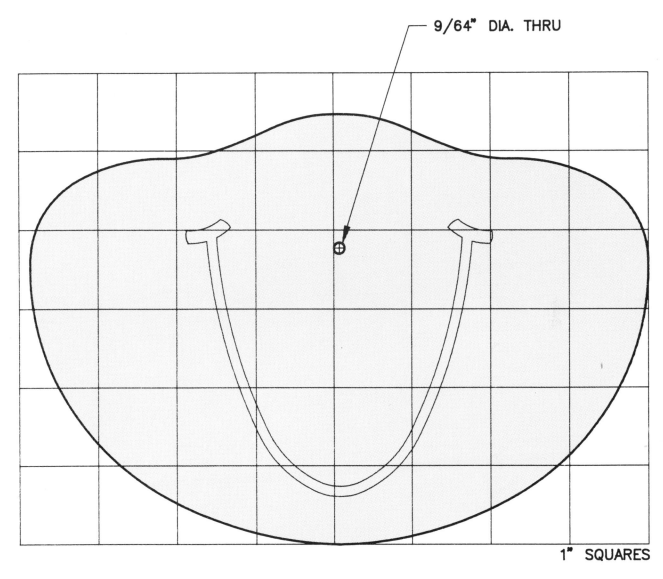

9/64" DIA. THRU

1" SQUARES

4-4. Muzzle.

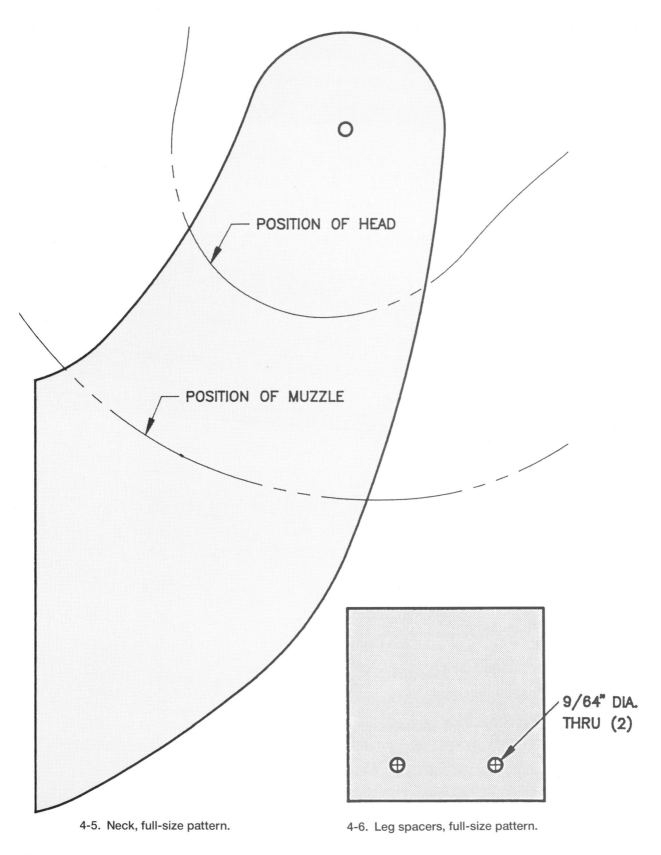

POSITION OF HEAD

POSITION OF MUZZLE

9/64" DIA. THRU (2)

4-5. Neck, full-size pattern.

4-6. Leg spacers, full-size pattern.

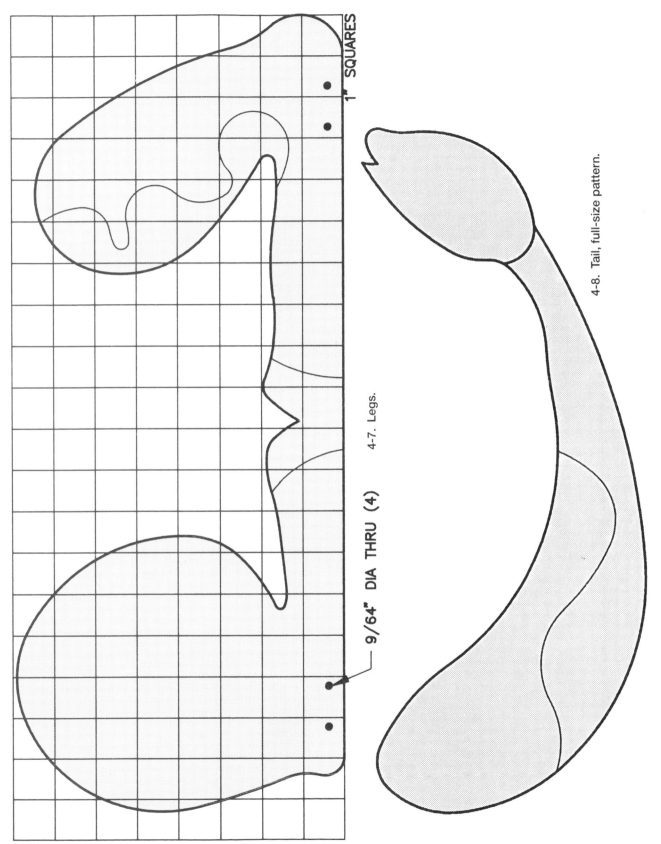

1" SQUARES

9/64" DIA THRU (4)

4-7. Legs.

4-8. Tail, full-size pattern.

41

5

Largemouth Bass

Fishing is one of the most popular hobbies in America. The largemouth bass is found in freshwater lakes and rivers in almost every state. This project consists primarily of ½″ and ¾″ stock that is cut, sanded, painted, and attached to a small-size mailbox. See the exploded assembly drawings, 5-2–5-4. Big, bulging plastic eyes add a nice finishing touch.

Table 5-1 lists all the materials required.

Baseboard, Tail, Spacer, and Eyes

Baseboard. Cut out the baseboard and attach it to the mailbox temporarily with one screw on each side. Remove the baseboard and set it aside.

Tail and Tail Spacer. Lay out the tail spacer (5-5) on ½″ stock and cut out. Drill two ¹¹⁄₆₄″ holes through, as specified.

After enlarging the tail (5-5), transfer it to ¾″ stock and cut out. Note the location of the pilot holes. Drill only one of these two pilot holes. Attach the tail spacer to the tail with one screw. Use the remaining hole in the tail spacer as a guide to drill the second pilot hole in the tail.

Disassemble the tail from the tail spacer. To drill matching holes through the back of the mailbox, place the tail spacer against the back of the mailbox and use it as a drilling guide. Drill two ¹¹⁄₆₄″ diameter holes.

The tail and tail spacer can now be attached to the mailbox from the inside with 2″ × #8 hex-head sheet metal screws and a socket wrench. See 5-2. Sheet metal screws with hex heads are recommended, because they can be driven with a socket wrench.

Eyes. The eyes are 1⁷⁄₁₆″ diameter plastic frog eyes. They are available at many craft stores. These eyes

have ¼″ diameter plastic mounting shanks. With this type of plastic eye, drill two ¼″ holes two inches back from the door and six inches up from the bottom of the mailbox on each side. Do not install the frog eyes until the mailbox has been fully painted. **Note:** The ¼″ shank holes for plastic eyes are not needed if you intend to paint eyes on the bass, another option.

Mouth and Dorsal Fin

Enlarge the designs (5-7–5-9) as necessary, then transfer the patterns to ¾″ stock and cut out. These pieces will be mounted to the mailbox with sheet metal screws. The approximate locations of the pilot holes are given only as a guide. Use the side-view drawing (5-6) as a guideline for positioning the mouth and dorsal fin.

Drill ¹¹⁄₆₄″ diameter mounting holes in the mailbox. Attach the mouth to the mailbox with ½″ × #8 sheet metal screws installed from the inside of the mailbox. Attach the dorsal fin in the same manner, using 1″ × #8 sheet metal screws.

Fins. Transfer the fin-spacer pattern (5-10) onto ½″ stock and cut out two pieces. Transfer the fin pattern (5-11) onto ¾″ stock and make a left- and right-hand piece. Drill holes in the fins and fin spacers as specified.

Using the fin spacer as a guide, mark and drill two ⁹⁄₆₄″ diameter holes through the bottom metal flange on each side of the mailbox. (See 5-6 for approximate location.) Reposition the baseboard under the mailbox and drill ⁷⁄₆₄″ pilot holes to attach the fin spacer and fin. Use 1⅝″ × #6 trim-head finishing screws.

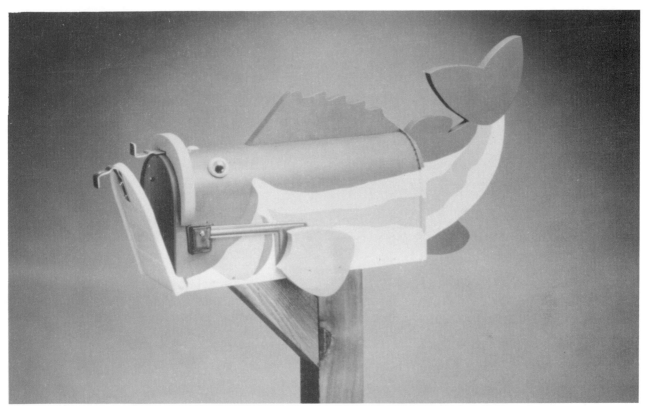

5-1. Among anglers, the largemouth bass is one of the most popular fish in North America.

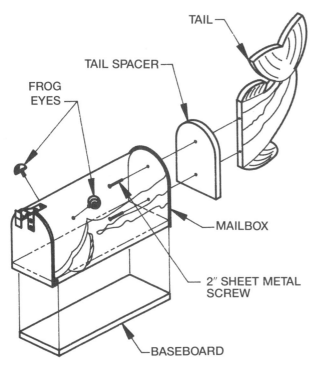

5-2. Exploded drawing shows the assembly of the frog eyes, tail spacer, and tail.

Table 5-1—List of Materials
(Dimensions are for a #1 or T1 mailbox)

Quantity	Part	Size of Material
1	Baseboard	*¾ × 6⅛ × 17½
2	Tail	¾ × 10⅝ × 16⅝
2	Tail spacer	¾ × 6⅛ × 8½
2	Mouth	¾ × 5⁹⁄₃₂ × 7¹⁵⁄₃₂
2	Dorsal fin	¾ × 3½ × 11½
2	Fin spacer	½ × 3⅜ × 5¾
2	Fin	¾ × 4⅞ × 5¾
2	Sheet metal screw	½ × #8
2	Sheet metal screw	1 × #8
2	Sheet metal screw	2 × #8
9	Sheet metal screw	⅝ × #6
2	Frog eye	1⁷⁄₁₆ dia.
4	Trim-head drywall screw	1⅝ × #6
1	White mailbox	Size #1 or T1

Recommended paint colors: white, red, light green, olive green, green, black.

*Size of baseboard may vary, depending on the brand of mailbox.

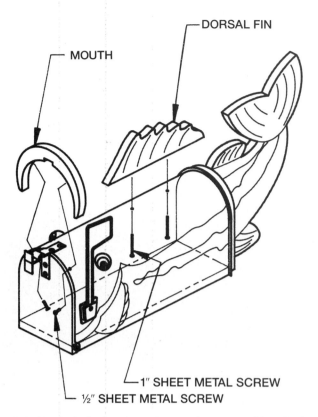

MOUTH

DORSAL FIN

1″ SHEET METAL SCREW

½″ SHEET METAL SCREW

5-3. Exploded drawing shows the assembly of the mouth and dorsal fin.

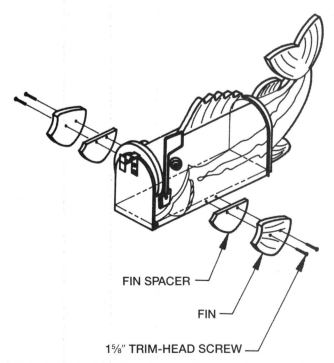

FIN SPACER

FIN

1⅝″ TRIM-HEAD SCREW

5-4. Exploded drawing showing the assembly of the fins and fin spacers.

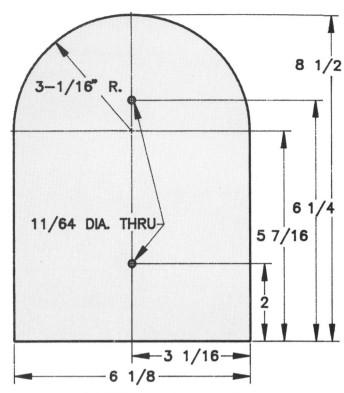

3–1/16″ R.

11/64 DIA. THRU

8 1/2

6 1/4

5 7/16

2

3 1/16

6 1/8

5-5. Tail-spacer layout details.

Final Assembly

Sanding and Painting. After all wood parts have been attached, remove them for final sanding and painting. Suggested colors are given in 5-6. See Chapter 1 for general painting tips.

Mounting the Mailbox. Attach the baseboard to the mailbox post. After painting, assemble all parts. If using plastic eyes, attach them at this time. Secure the eyes with silicone glue applied around the shank of the eye on the inside of the mailbox.

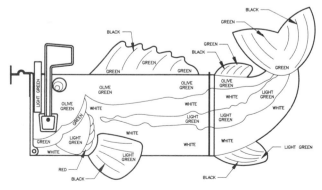

5-6. Painting guide.

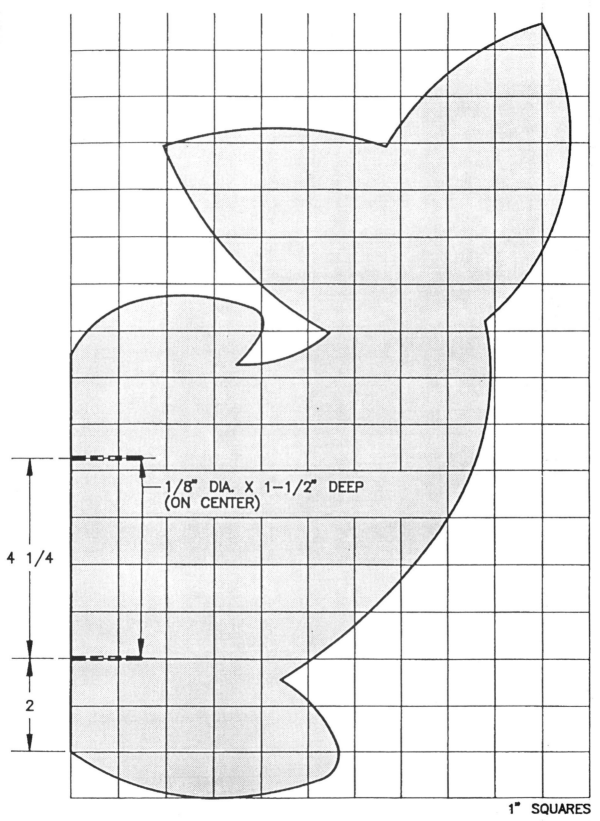

1/8" DIA. X 1–1/2" DEEP
(ON CENTER)

4 1/4

2

1" SQUARES

5-7. Tail detail.

45

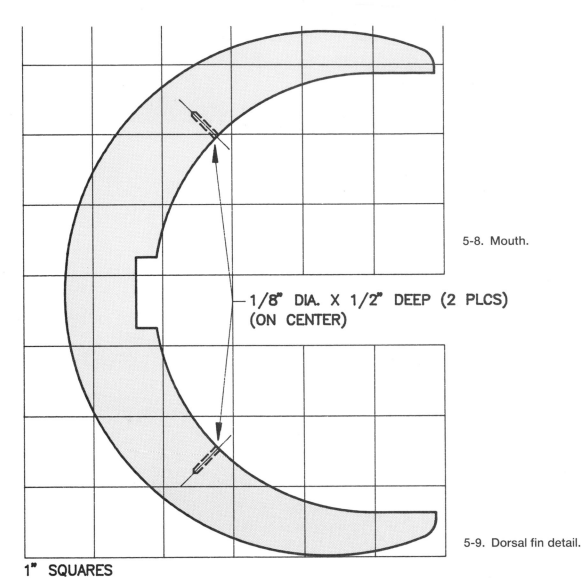

5-8. Mouth.

1/8" DIA. X 1/2" DEEP (2 PLCS)
(ON CENTER)

5-9. Dorsal fin detail.

1" SQUARES

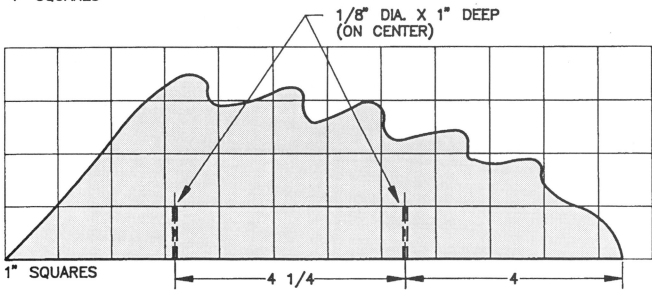

1/8" DIA. X 1" DEEP
(ON CENTER)

1" SQUARES

4 1/4

4

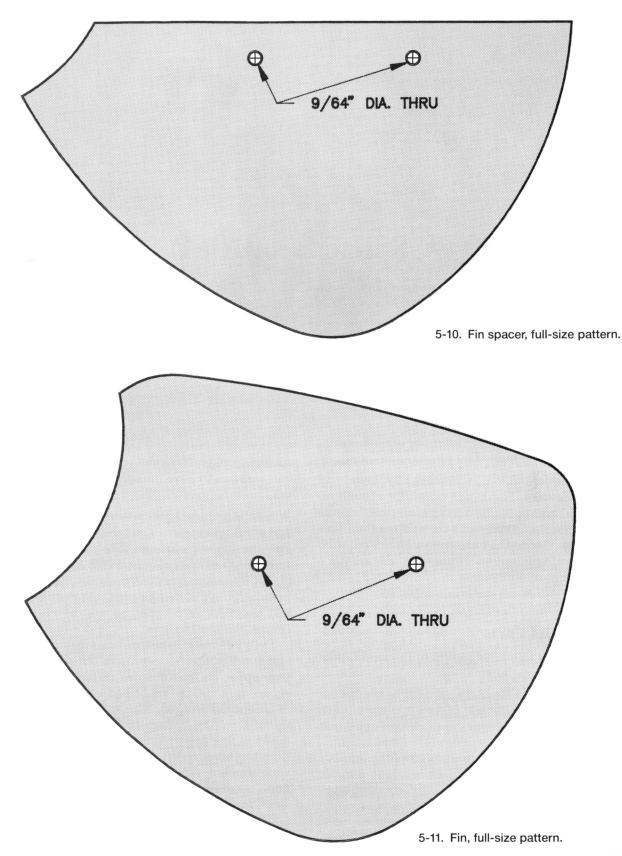

9/64" DIA. THRU

5-10. Fin spacer, full-size pattern.

9/64" DIA. THRU

5-11. Fin, full-size pattern.

Next, remove the wing and redrill just the two upper holes in each side of the mailbox, enlarging them to ¹¹⁄₆₄″. Reattach the wing with ½″ sheet metal screws, and fill the holes in the surfaces of the wings with wood putty.

Tip: Place a washer under the head of each of the ½″ sheet metal screws, so the tips of the screws do not come back through the wings.

An alternate method of driving the screws into the wings is as follows: First, remove the two lower screws holding the wings. Mark and drill the ¹¹⁄₆₄″ holes into the mailbox. Reattach the wings and mark through the upper set of holes from the inside with a pencil or awl. Then remove the wings and drill ⅛″ pilot holes ⁷⁄₁₆″ deep into the back surface of the wing. This method eliminates the need to fill holes with wood putty.

Feet. Cut two feet from ½″ exterior plywood (6-6). Drill ¹¹⁄₆₄″ clearance holes in the mailbox door; then, with the feet positioned on the outside of the door, mark the location of the pilot hole with a pencil or scratch awl. Drill ⅛″ holes about ⁷⁄₁₆″ deep into the feet. Fasten the feet to the door with ½″ × #8 sheet metal screws. Placing a washer under the head of each screw assures that the screw tips do not penetrate all the way through the feet.

Finishing

Sanding. Remove all wood pieces and finish-sand. Fill any voids in the plywood wings and feet with wood putty.

Painting. Begin with a white mailbox or paint it yourself. Paint the top grey, as shown on color page A. Prime all wood parts, and paint according to the color recommendations on 6-4 and 6-7. Paint the feet orange.

Final Assembly. Reattach all pieces to the mailbox with screws. Touch up the heads of the screws with paint so they blend in.

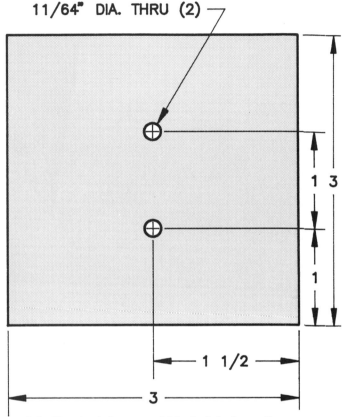

6-3. Head-reinforcement block, full-size pattern.

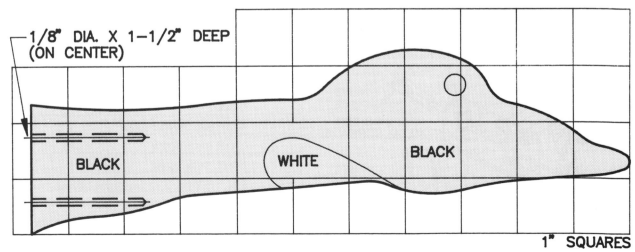

6-4. Head detail.

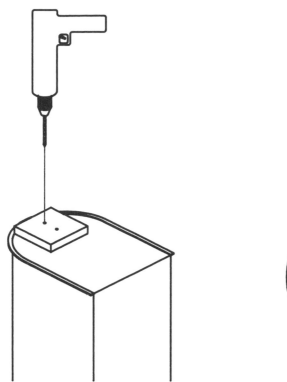

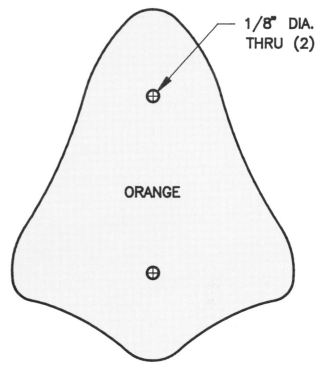

1/8" DIA.
THRU (2)

6-5. Position the head-reinforcement block on the out-side back of the mailbox, and use it as a guide to drill two $^{11}/_{64}$" clearance holes through the mailbox.

6-6. Foot, full-size pattern.

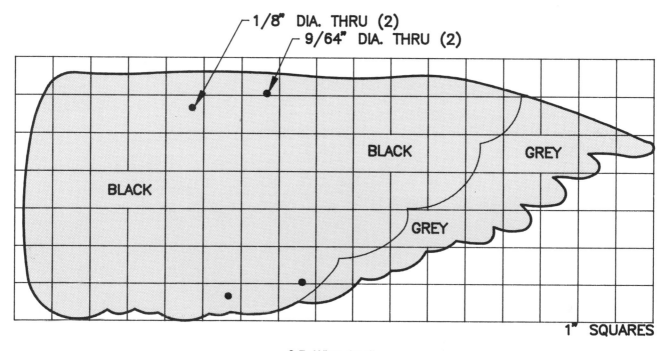

1/8" DIA. THRU (2)
9/64" DIA. THRU (2)

BLACK

BLACK

GREY

BLACK

GREY

1" SQUARES

6-7. Wing detail.

7
Ducks in a Row

Five different mailbox ducks sitting in a row. The perfect solution for decorating multiple mailboxes. Of course, any of these designs can be used alone.

Although it would not take too much time to make all five variations yourself and just give them to the neighbors, try to get several of your neighbors involved in the project. One could build a new stand; another could help with the painting. Maybe those who aren't handy could donate money for materials or plan a neighborhood get-together for the day the mailboxes are installed.

The heads are mounted on the back of the mailbox, which completely eliminates any interference with the operation of the door. See the exploded assembly drawings, 7-2–7-4. Except for the heads, all the parts are identical. This makes it very easy to make the entire set.

Table 7-1 lists all materials required.

Cutting the Parts

Baseboard. Cut the baseboard to fit the mailbox(es), but do not fasten it.

Head and Wings. Select the duck head (or heads). See 7-5–7-9. Enlarge and cut out the patterns from ½″ exterior plywood. Cut a left and right wing for each mailbox, making sure the better side faces out. See 7-10.

Wing Spacers, Head Spacer, Tail, and Feet. Cut these parts from ½″ plywood, using a band saw or scroll saw. Sand all edges as necessary.

Mounting the Head and Head Spacer

The purpose of the head spacer is to keep the head away from the protruding flange on the back of the mailbox.

The holes specified (7-12) are for attaching with 1″ × #8 sheet metal screws. Drill ¹¹⁄₆₄″ holes in the head spacer. Position the head spacer on the back of the mailbox and use it as a drilling template to drill ¹¹⁄₆₄″ holes through the back of the mailbox.

Install the sheet metal screws from inside the mailbox, through the ¹¹⁄₆₄″ holes in the back of the mailbox, through the head spacer, and finally into the head. *Note:* For simplicity, we have suggested drilling the pilot holes all the way through the head(s). This allows the head(s) to be mounted facing either left or right. You may wish instead to drill the ⅛″ pilot holes just ⁷⁄₁₆″ deep from only one side. This eliminates the need to fill holes with wood putty prior to painting.

Tip: A 1″ sheet metal screw extends nearly through the surface of the head. Place a flat washer under the screw head as a preventive measure.

Plastic Eyes. To install plastic animal eyes, drill ¼″ diameter shank holes all the way through the thickness of all heads—except the head style that looks straight up. The shanks may have to be shortened in length so they will not touch one another when two eyes are installed through the same hole (one on each side). Do not install the plastic eyes until the head is painted. Shank holes for plastic eyes are not needed if you are going to paint the eyes yourself.

Mounting the Wings and Spacers

Wing spacers, like the head spacer, are attached with 1″ × #8 sheet metal screws. They are also drilled with ¹¹⁄₆₄″ clearance holes all the way through.

The purpose of the wing spacer is to allow

7-1. This "Ducks in a Row" project is the perfect way to give multiple mailboxes a country motif.

enough space on the flag side of the mailbox for the flag to operate normally. For symmetry, put a wing spacer on the other side of the mailbox, too.

Drill 11⁄64″ holes in each of the wing spacers (7-13). After drilling the wing spacers, locate their position on the sides of the mailbox, as shown in 7-12. Use the wing spacer as a drilling template and drill the 11⁄64″ holes through the sides of the mailbox.

Position the wing as desired on the side of the mailbox and mark the location of the pilot holes in the wing. Using a scratch awl or pencil, mark through the 11⁄64″ holes from inside the mailbox.

Drill 1⁄8″ pilot holes into the back surface of each wing (about 7⁄16″ deep). Install the wing spacers and wings. When making several ducks, consider positioning the wings upward slightly on one or more of them for variety.

If using a 1″ screw, use a washer under the screw head to prevent the screw from penetrating all the way through the wing.

Mounting the Tail

The tail (7-14) is mounted directly to the front of the mailbox door. Position the tail so it is centered

Table 7-1—List of Materials
(Dimensions are for a #1 or T1 rural mailbox)

Quantity	Part	Size of Material
1	Baseboard	*3⁄4 × 6 1⁄8 × 17 1⁄2
1	Head spacer	1⁄2 × 6 1⁄8 × 6 1⁄8
1	Head	1⁄2 × (see patterns)
2	Wing	1⁄2 × 6 1⁄8 × 11 3⁄8
2	Wing spacer	1⁄2 × 2 × 2 3⁄4
1	Foot	1⁄2 × 4 5⁄8 × 4 3⁄8
1	Foot	1⁄2 × 4 1⁄4 × 4 3⁄4
1	Tail	1⁄2 × 3 × 4 1⁄2
2	Sheet metal screw	1⁄2 × #8
6	Sheet metal screw	1 × #8
9	Sheet metal screw	5⁄8 × #6
2	Plastic eye	1 5⁄8 w/1⁄4 shank
2	Drywall screw	2 × #6
1	White mailbox	Size #1 or T1

Recommended exterior enamel paint colors: white, yellow, orange, black.

*Size of baseboard may vary, depending on the brand of mailbox.

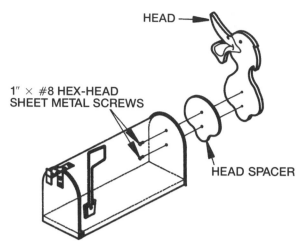

HEAD

1″ × #8 HEX-HEAD
SHEET METAL SCREWS

HEAD SPACER

7-2. Exploded assembly drawing, showing the installation of the head and the head spacer.

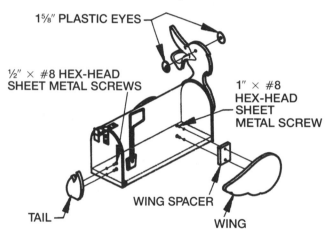

1⅝″ PLASTIC EYES

½″ × #8 HEX-HEAD
SHEET METAL SCREWS

1″ × #8
HEX-HEAD
SHEET
METAL SCREW

TAIL

WING SPACER

WING

7-3. Exploded assembly drawing, showing the installation of wings, wing spacers, tail, and plastic eyes.

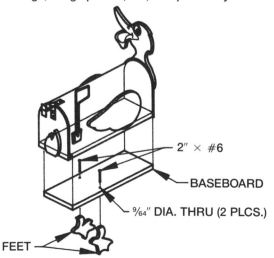

2″ × #6

BASEBOARD

⁹⁄₆₄″ DIA. THRU (2 PLCS.)

FEET

7-4. Exploded assembly drawing, showing the feet mounted to the baseboard.

on the door, with the flat side even with the bottom of the door. Drill two ¹¹⁄₆₄″ diameter holes in the door, then mark and drill ⅛″ diameter pilot holes in the tail. Drill these pilot holes ⁷⁄₆₄″ deep. Mount the tail, using two ½″ × #8 sheet metal screws with a flat washer under each screw head.

Finishing

Remove all wood parts from the mailbox and finish-sand. Using wood putty, fill any voids in the center plies of the plywood. Prime and paint the pieces white. Paint the duck bills the colors shown in the head drawings. If you are painting eyes on the head, do so now. Paint the duck feet yellow.

If using plastic shank eyes, use a hammer to tap the eyes into the ¼″ holes. If the ¼″ shanks on the back of each eye do not fit tightly, add some epoxy or silicone adhesive.

If you are not using a white, prepainted mailbox, paint yours at this time. See Chapter 1 for painting tips.

Final Assembly

Reassemble all parts on the mailbox. If you are using a single wood post, nail the feet directly to it. Otherwise, attach the feet to the baseboard with 2″ × #6 screws before securing the mailbox to the baseboard. See 7-4. Chapter 1 shows ways of mounting the feet using different kinds of posts and presents options for mounting one or a series of duck mailboxes. See 1-54.

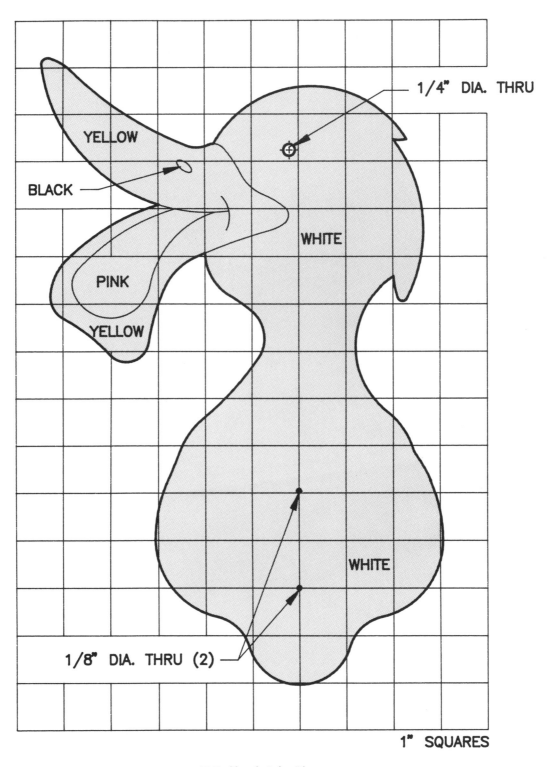

1/4" DIA. THRU

YELLOW

BLACK

PINK

YELLOW

WHITE

WHITE

1/8" DIA. THRU (2)

1" SQUARES

7-5. Head style #1.

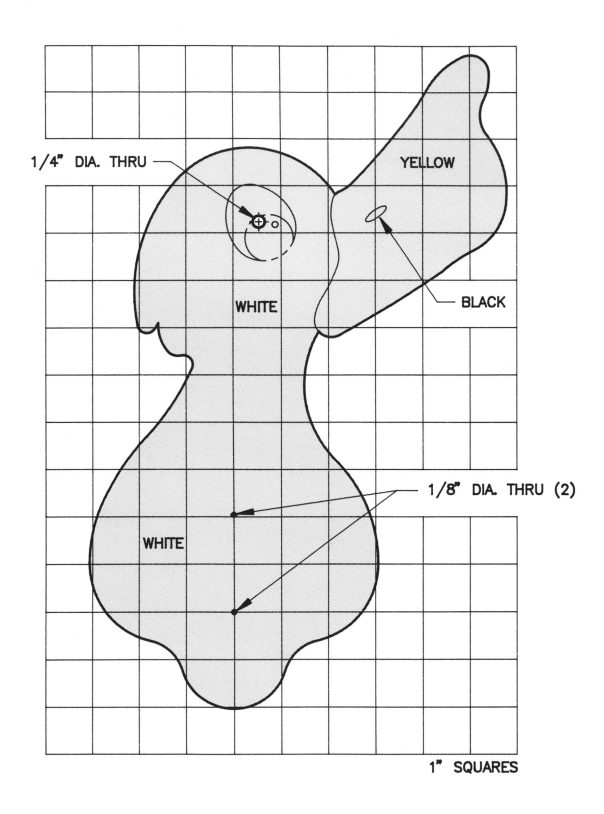

1/4" DIA. THRU

YELLOW

BLACK

WHITE

1/8" DIA. THRU (2)

WHITE

1" SQUARES

7-6. Head style #2.

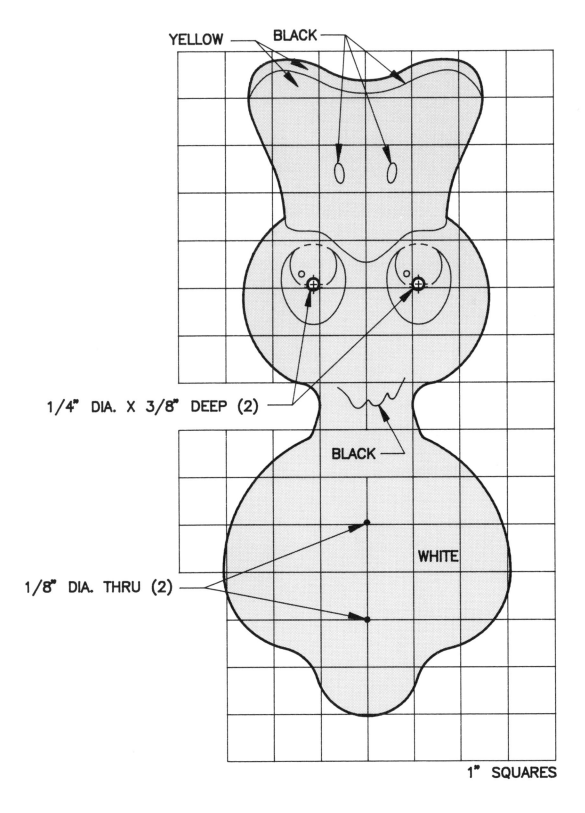

YELLOW · BLACK

BLACK

1/4" DIA. X 3/8" DEEP (2)

WHITE

1/8" DIA. THRU (2)

1" SQUARES

7-7. Head style #3.

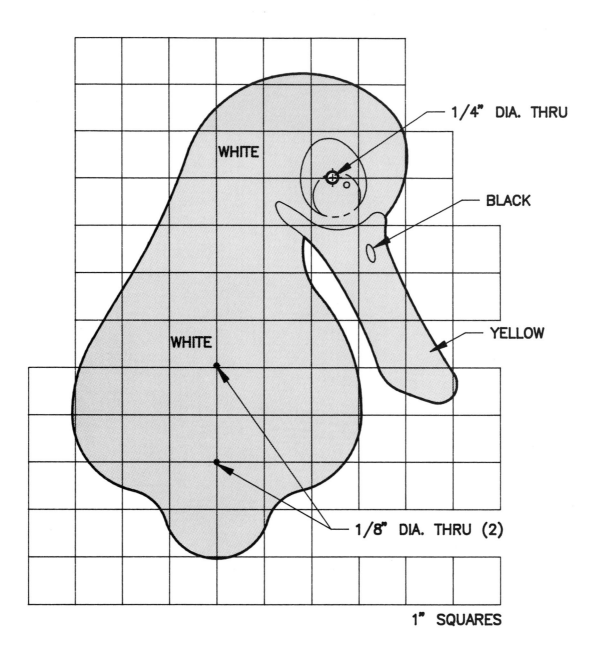

1/4" DIA. THRU

BLACK

YELLOW

WHITE

WHITE

1/8" DIA. THRU (2)

1" SQUARES

7-8. Head style #4.

58

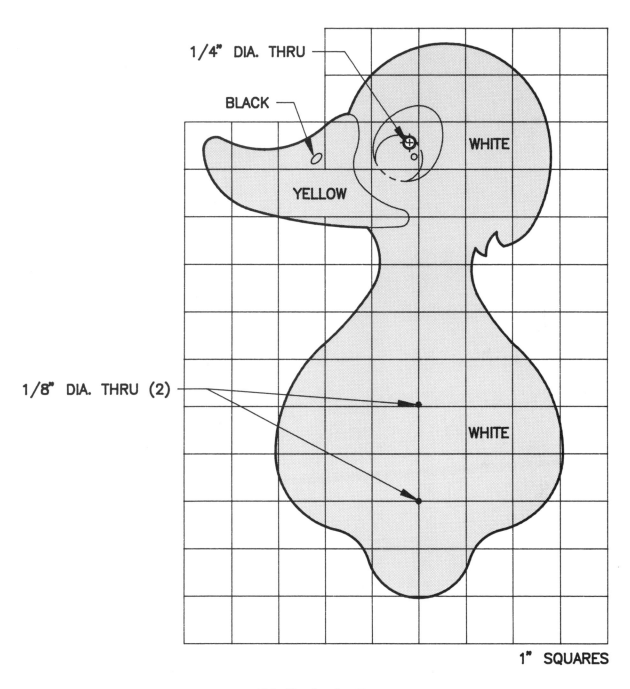

1/4" DIA. THRU

BLACK

WHITE

YELLOW

1/8" DIA. THRU (2)

WHITE

1" SQUARES

7-9. Head style #5.

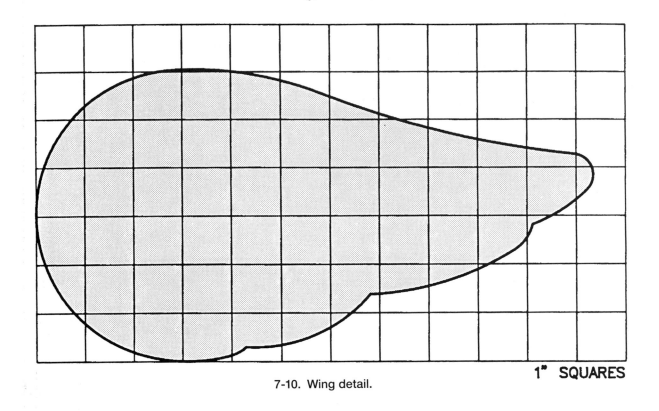

7-10. Wing detail.

1" SQUARES

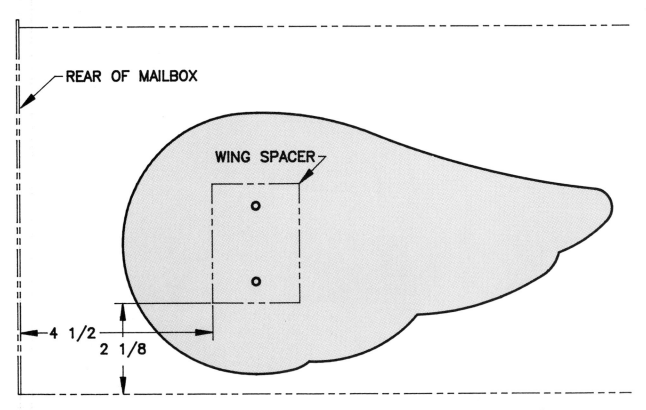

REAR OF MAILBOX

WING SPACER

4 1/2

2 1/8

7-11. The location of the wing and wing spacer, as mounted from the rear of the mailbox.

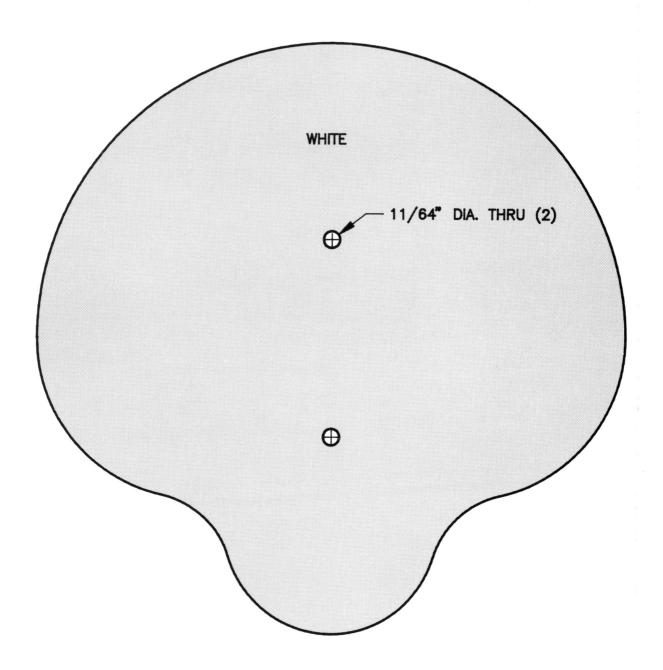

WHITE

11/64" DIA. THRU (2)

7-12. Head spacer, full-size pattern.

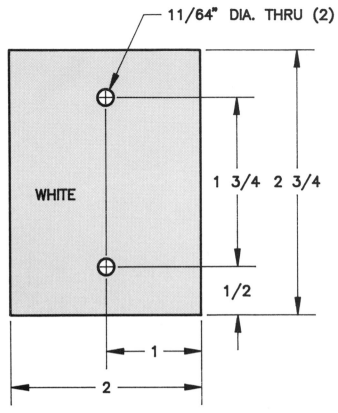

11/64" DIA. THRU (2)

WHITE

1 3/4   2 3/4

1/2

1

2

7-13. Wing spacer.

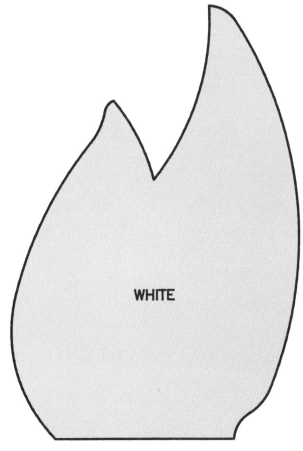

WHITE

7-14. Tail, full-size pattern.

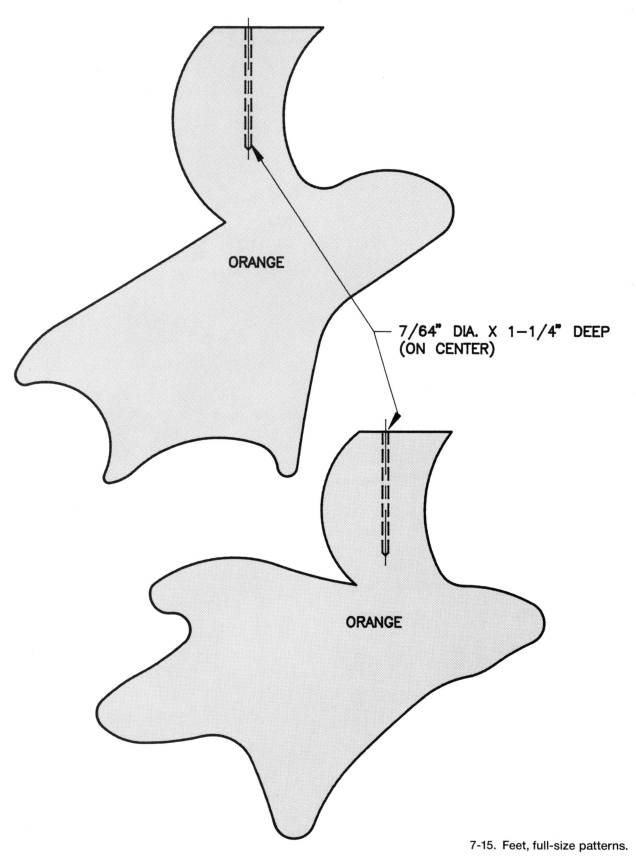

ORANGE

7/64" DIA. X 1—1/4" DEEP
(ON CENTER)

ORANGE

7-15. Feet, full-size patterns.

8

Four Fun Vehicles

The mailbox is perfect for creating your own sculpture of a car, truck, tractor, or even a fire engine! After all, the shape of a mailbox looks a lot like the hood of an old-fashioned vehicle. It is easy to imagine the mailbox as the basis for motor vehicles of almost any conceivable shape or description. The front of the mailbox actually serves as the vehicle's hood, so a portion of the vehicle is already there. All that needs to be added are the sides of the vehicle and the wheels. If you wish, a driver can be chosen from a variety of designs that are also included in this chapter.

The four mailbox vehicle designs presented here share a number of similar construction details. They all use the same fenders, doors, wheels, axles, and optional drivers. The following information applies to the tractor mailbox in Chapter 9 as well as these four fun vehicles.

Materials. All the parts for the vehicles are made from readily available materials. The two sides are made from ½″ exterior plywood. The fenders are made from ¾″ plywood or solid stock.

Doors are shown in the drawings of the car, pickup truck, and fire truck. They can be cut from a piece of ¼″ plywood or hardboard and nailed or glued onto the side pieces of each vehicle. Or, draw the outline of the door directly on the side of the vehicle. Use a pinstripe brush, a felt-tip pen or paint marker, or apply ⅛″ wide automotive striping tape. This tape is available from automotive supply stores and some hardware stores.

Wheels

Here are three possibilities for wheels: 1) Make them from a single piece of solid wood and paint the details on; 2) Make them from two scroll-sawed layers of plywood and add realistic detail; 3) Purchase them from a hardware store or mail-order supply source.

Making Wheels from Solid Stock. Wheels can be cut from 1½″ thick redwood, fir, or any 2″ structural planks. See 8-5. Remember that nominal 2″ dimension stock is always less than its specified size. If you want to make a 6″ diameter wheel, use a piece of 2 × 8 stock (which really measures about 1½ inches thick by 7½ inches wide).

To lay out wheels on "two by" stock, simply mark a circle with a compass. *Tip:* Before cutting, enlarge the tiny hole left by the compass point with a scratch awl. This makes it easier to find the center when you are ready to drill the axle hole.

When sawing the wheels, be sure to cut on the waste side of the line, leaving some material on the perimeter to sand smooth later.

Drill the center hole to fit whatever size axle you will be using. A ¼″ axle is adequate for a steel or fibreglass axle. For a wood-dowel axle, use at least a ½″ diameter for strength. To make perfectly round wheels, sand each one on a disc sander while rotating the wheel around a pivot pin in the axle hole.

Painting center designs and spokes on the face of the wheel gives a more realistic look. See 8-5.

Layered Plywood Wheels. A more detailed wheel can be made using two pieces of ½″ plywood cut to the appropriate diameter. See 8-6–8-7. Enlarge the wheel and spoke layout shown in 8-8 to match the diameter of the wheel.

Eight-inch wheels are used on all the cars and trucks. The tractor specifies 6″ and 10″ wheels.

8-1. Pickup truck.

8-2. Fire truck.

8-3. Car with rumble seat.

8-4. Delivery truck.

With the "enlargement by squares" technique, the 1″ grid pattern gives an 8″ diameter wheel. Use a photocopier to create patterns for 6″ or 10″ wheels.

Use a scroll saw to remove the pie-shaped sections that form the spokes on the outside layer. See 8-6. (It is not necessary to cut spokes in the bottom, or backing, layer.) Sand the cut-out spoke areas as necessary, then glue the two plywood discs together. After the glue dries, drill the axle hole and true the outside circumference on a disc sander. A final, optional, step: Round the outside edges using a router and a ¼″ radius round-over bit.

Using Purchased Wheels. Factory-made wheels are available from hardware stores and mail-order woodworking supply catalogs. See 8-9. These range from inexpensive, all-plastic construction to high-quality steel wheels with real rubber tread and ball-bearing centers. Select a wheel that is compatible with the project.

Mounting the Wheels. All the vehicles have side pieces with areas protruding below the bottom of the mailbox for the axles. See 8-10. Although the plans specify ½″ holes, be sure to make the axle

8-5. Painting the wheel detail on a solid wheel cut from 1½″ thick stock.

8-7. The completed wheel, made from two layers of ½″ plywood.

8-6. Use a scroll saw to remove the center, pie-shaped sections from the outer layer. *Note:* The large entry holes bored into the waste permit the blade to be threaded without removing it from the blade clamp.

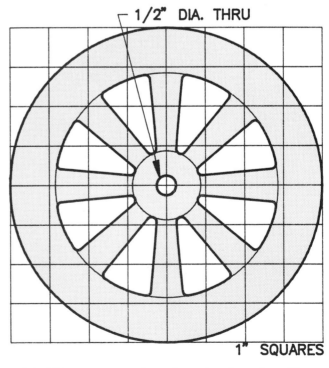

1/2″ DIA. THRU

1″ SQUARES

8-8. This pattern can be enlarged and used as either a paint pattern (8-5) or a cutting pattern (8-6). The wheel has a ½ × 8″ diameter.

8-9. These wheels can be purchased at a moderate price. They are available in all the sizes required for the projects in Chapters 8 and 9.

holes about ¹⁄₆₄″ larger than the diameter of the axle. Wheel-hole and -axle combinations may range anywhere upward from ¼″ diameter, depending upon style and availability.

To install the wheels, either bolt them directly to the side piece of the vehicle using just a nut and bolt (8-10), or use steel, fibreglass, or wood axle rods, as shown in 8-11. It makes no difference whether or not the wheels actually turn.

Friction axle caps, or "push-on nuts," can be used on the ends of the axles to secure the wheels. Another method is to drill a hole in the end of the axle and use a cotter pin and washer. See 8-11.

Delivery Truck

General Instructions. Because the four vehicles presented here are so similar, the procedures described for building the delivery truck can be applied to making the others.

All four vehicles in this chapter share exactly the same fenders, side spacers, wheels, and axle specifications. They also are all built around the small size (No. 1 or T1) rural mailbox.

Table 8-1 is the list of materials for the delivery truck. The lists of materials and necessary drawings for building the car, pickup truck, and fire truck are given later in the chapter.

Delivery Truck Baseboard and Sides

Baseboard. Cut the baseboard to fit the recess opening under the mailbox. See Chapter 1.

Side Spacers. Cut two ½ × 1 × 15½″ side spacers (Ref. #2 in Table 8-1). The spacers set the sides of

8-10. A wheel bolted directly to side piece of the vehicle.

8-11. Wheels can be mounted with a wood, fibreglass, or steel axle. Use push nuts (*right*) to lock wheels in place, or drill a hole in the end of each axle and secure it, using a cotter pin (*left*).

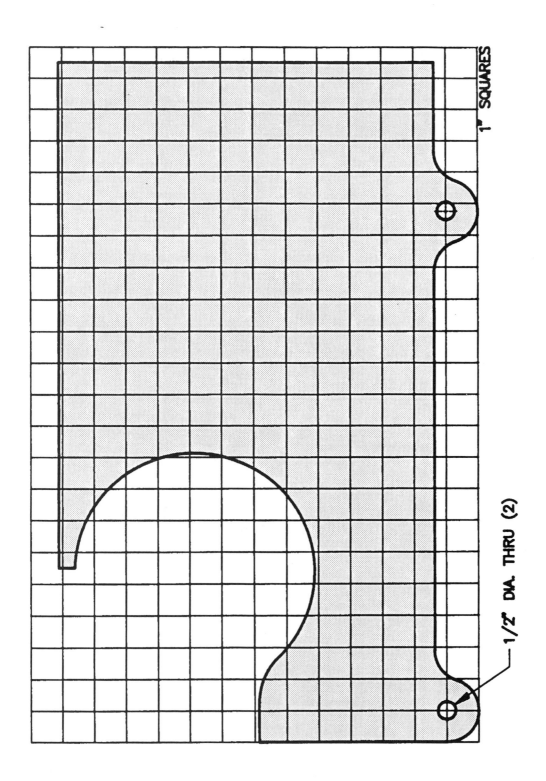

1" SQUARES

1/2" DIA. THRU (2)

8-12. Side plan for the delivery truck. Enlarge as required. Side plans for the pickup truck, fire truck, and car are on pages 77, 79, and 81, respectively.

the vehicle away from the sides of the metal mailbox. This ensures clearance for the flag to operate smoothly.

Side Pieces. The shape of the side pieces is different for each vehicle. See 8-12 for the plan of the side pieces for the delivery truck mailbox. The photos in 8-13–8-17 show the major steps in making and installing the side pieces for the delivery truck. Follow the same general procedure for the car, pickup truck, and fire truck mailboxes. See 8-32, 8-38, and 8-44 for the plans for making the sides of these three vehicles.

There are two methods for laying out and cutting the side pieces. The first method, "stack cutting," is the process of holding two or more pieces together, one on top of the other, and sawing them all at the same time. Simply nail them together in the waste area. In 8-13, two pieces of plywood are stacked with the best side of each piece positioned face to face, to prevent chipping on the good side of the plywood, and to give identical left- and right-side pieces.

In 8-13, the pattern has been transferred to the back of the top piece of plywood. Mark the location of the axle holes with a scratch awl and drill before sawing the parts.

An alternate method, which works well with a light-duty saw, such as a scroll saw or sabre saw, is to lay out and cut each piece individually. In this case, remember to place the left and right sides so the best side of the plywood faces out. When transferring the pattern, be sure to mark the holes for the axles in each piece with a scratch awl.

Quantity	Ref. #	Part	Size of Material
1	1	Baseboard	*¾ × 6⅛ × 17½
2	2	Side spacers	½ × 1 × 15½
2	3	Sides	½ × 13⅛ × 21½
2	4	Fenders	¾ × 6⅜ × 24¼
1	5	Roof	½ × 8 × 17
1	6	Driver	3 dia. wood ball
2	7	Axle	½ dia. × 12
4	8	Axle cap	½ push nut
4	9	Wheel	8 dia.
Misc.	10	Screws	As needed
1	11	Mailbox	Size #1 or T1

Table 8-1—List of Materials
(Dimensions are for a #1 or T1 rural mailbox)

*Size of baseboard may vary, depending on the brand of mailbox.

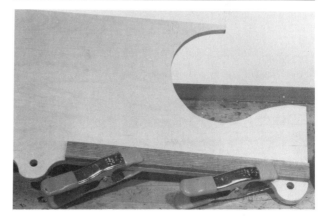

8-14. Glue the narrow spacer strips flush with the front edge and even with the bottom edge, as shown.

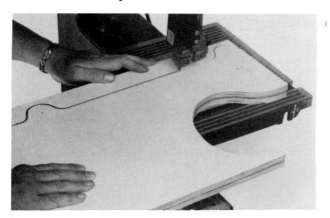

8-13. Stack-cutting both side pieces on a band saw for the delivery truck. Note that the location of the axle holes is marked with a scratch awl when the design is transferred to the plywood. The axle holes can be drilled before the pieces are sawed.

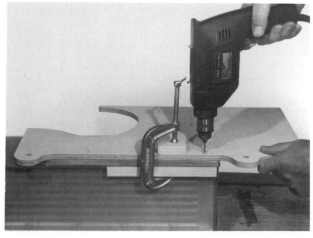

8-15. Drilling clearance holes through the plywood side and through the metal lip of the mailbox.

69

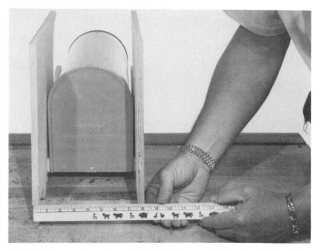

8-16. Measuring the width of the vehicle to determine the finished size of the top piece.

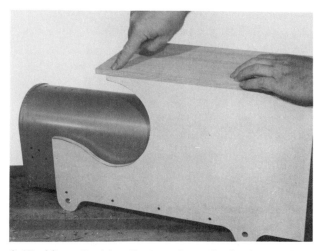

8-17. After attaching the top piece, the basic structure for the delivery truck is finished. Remember to check the list of materials for the length of the top piece. The top extends over the body on some vehicles.

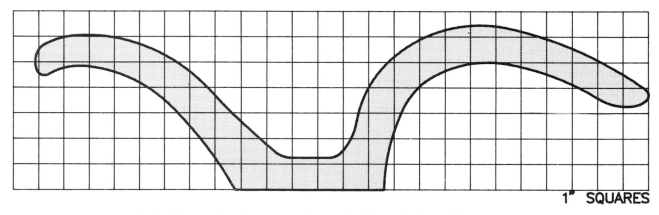

1" SQUARES

8-18. This fender plan is used for each of the vehicles in this chapter.

8-19. With the wheels in place, center the fender between the wheels.

Note: For the car, pickup truck, or the fire truck, also mark the location of the ½″ diameter holes for the windshield support.

After the side pieces are cut and sanded and the holes drilled, attach the side spacers. Glue the spacers to the *inside* of each of the side pieces, as shown in 8-14. Spacers should be positioned along the inside straight bottom edge of each side piece with one end flush with the front end of the side piece. Use water-resistant glue.

Once the spacer strips are secured, drill three holes on each side, to attach the side pieces to the mailbox. With the baseboard removed, clamp one of the side pieces to the mailbox for drilling, as shown in 8-15. Note that the straight bottom edge should be even with the bottom of the mailbox and the plywood side positioned as far back as possible, so the end of the spacer stops at the rear lip of the metal mailbox.

After all holes have been drilled on both sides, reposition the baseboard in the recess under the metal mailbox, and fasten the side pieces with 2¼″ × #6 trim-head finishing screws.

Making the Top and Inside Pieces. The three trucks (delivery truck, pickup, and fire truck) each have a flat roof. The car has a flat-top support connecting the tops of the windshield supports. Even though the top pieces are attached in the same manner, the size of each piece is different. The width of each of these pieces depends on the assembled width of the mailbox and the thickness of material used to make the sides and side spacers. To determine the precise assembled width, measure as shown in 8-16. *Note:* For an accurate measurement, the sides must be parallel. Cut pieces for the flat-style roof tops so that the width of the top piece is equal to the assembled outside dimension. They should be approximately 8 inches.

Refer to the list of materials (Table 8-1) for the length of the top. The top of each vehicle overhangs in the front. The top of the delivery truck, shown in 8-17, is cut 17″ long.

Attach the top piece (or the crossbar, for the car) with screws. This completes the basic structure for making any one of the four vehicles in this chapter. All vehicles still need fenders, wheels, driver, and other special parts.

Fenders. The fenders are identical for each of the four vehicles. Enlarge the drawing (8-18), and cut a left and right side set of fenders. Be sure the best surfaces will face outward when assembled. The fenders can be cut from ¾″ plywood or solid stock. After cutting and sanding, the fenders should be temporarily installed with wood screws. To determine the best location for the fenders, lay the vehicle on its side. Position the wheels over their axle holes, and locate the bottom of the fender even with the bottom edge of the side of the vehicle (8-19). Move the fender left or right, until it looks evenly spaced between the wheels. Secure it with two wood screws.

Seat Board and Windshield Support. For the car, pickup truck, or fire truck, cut and install a seat board. This adds structural support and provides a platform the driver can be attached to. The seat board width must fit the project. The dowel for the windshield support can be cut to length now, but do not glue it in place yet. *Note:* The pickup truck has a tailgate and bed sides, and the car has a rumble seat. Cut and attach these pieces now. Remember, these parts should be cut to fit the inside width of the vehicle, so actual dimensions may vary slightly. For the fire truck, make the ladders and siren parts but don't attach them until later.

Vehicle Drivers

Little drivers will add personality to these vehicles. Because the three trucks all have roofs, the amount of headroom for the driver is limited. Measure the clearance, then select a driver design and size it to fit. Here are several methods of making mailbox drivers:

2 × 4 People. The simplest drivers are made from a short length of 2 × 4 stock. See 8-20. Transfer the outside profile of the figure to your stock. In the pickup truck, fire truck, car, and tractor mailboxes, the bottom of the driver should be flat, so he can be attached to the seat board. In the case of the delivery truck and some other mailboxes, such as the single-wing airplane, the 2 × 4 driver can be mounted directly to the top of the mailbox. For these projects, cut an arch on the bottom of the drivers, so they conform to the shape of the top of the mailbox.

The driver shown in 8-20 has ½″ wide × ⅜″ thick arms attached to each side. After sanding, glue the arms in place, prime, and paint.

Wood-Ball People. Another method of making drivers is to use a round wood ball for the driver's head. A 3″ diameter wood ball can be painted and

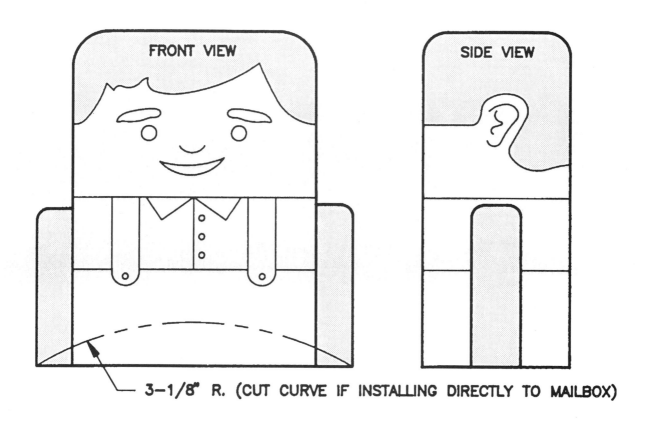

FRONT VIEW

SIDE VIEW

3–1/8" R. (CUT CURVE IF INSTALLING DIRECTLY TO MAILBOX)

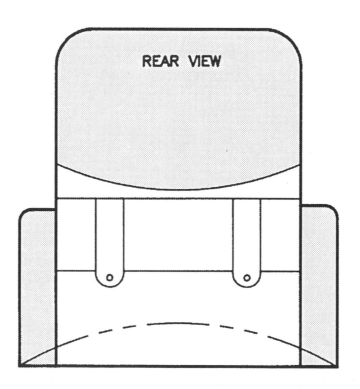

REAR VIEW

8-20. Full-size patterns for a 2 × 4 driver. Cut the head and body 1½ × 2½ × 3½". Cut two arms ⅜ × ½ × 1⅝".

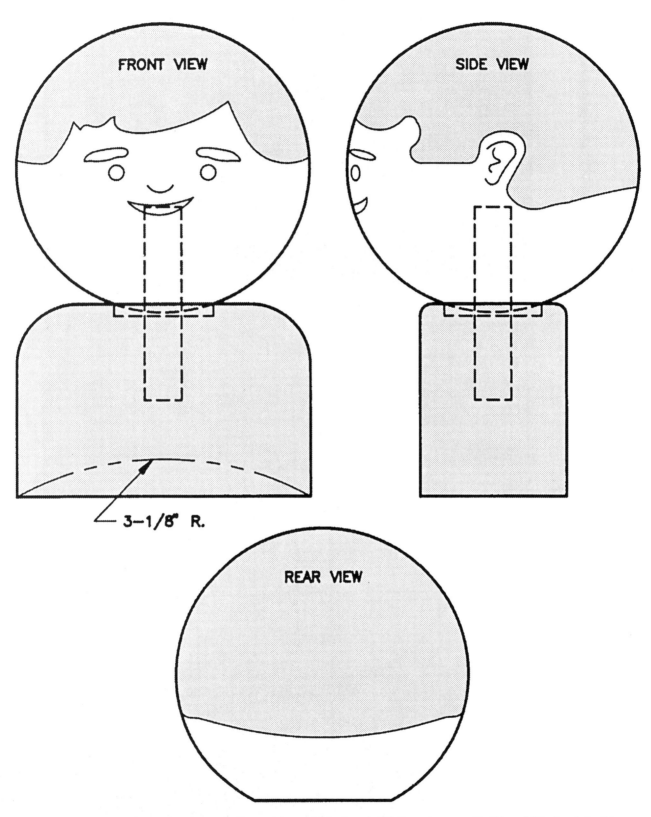

FRONT VIEW

SIDE VIEW

3-1/8" R.

REAR VIEW

8-21. This vehicle driver is made from a piece of 2 × 4 and a 3″ diameter wood ball head. The body is 1½ × 2 × 3″. The dowel pin is ⅜″ diameter × 2″.

mounted directly to the top of the mailbox, as is done on the delivery truck, shown in 8-4. (A similar ball "pilot" is used on the single-wing airplane, page 99). Round balls can be mounted directly to the mailbox with a sheet metal screw.

You can also give these wood-ball "people" shoulders. Cut a piece of 2 × 4 stock, as shown in 8-21–8-22. A shallow 1″ diameter hole bored in the top of the shoulder piece provides a perfect recessed area in which the wood ball can sit. A ⅜″ dowel pin is the preferred method of fastening the head to the shoulder piece. See 8-22.

Round wood balls of many sizes are available from mail order catalogs. One of the advantages of using solid round-ball heads is that it is easy to add felt or straw doll hats for an extra-special touch. See 8-23.

Using Doll Heads. An alternative to a wood-ball driver is a plastic doll's head. These are available from craft and toy stores. Look for a head proportional to the project. It may be necessary to detach the head and devise a way to mount it. If the head is hollow, a long bolt can be positioned with the threaded end sticking out the bottom of the neck. Fill the hollow head with plaster of paris or epoxy putty.

Finishing

Remove all wood pieces and finish-sand. Fill any voids with wood putty. Separate the fenders from the vehicle body for easier painting. See 8-24. Painting the fenders a contrasting color makes them stand out visibly. See Chapter 1 for tips on priming and painting.

Add special finishing touches, such as mailbox numbers or stripes, using automotive striping tape. See 8-25–8-26.

Final Assembly

After all pieces are painted, assemble all the parts. First, screw the baseboard to your mailbox post and then attach the mailbox, the vehicle body assembly, the fenders, and all other "add-ons." If a driver is to be included, attach it to the seat or directly to the top of the mailbox.

The final step is to install the wheels with nuts and bolts (8-10), or use axles (8-11).

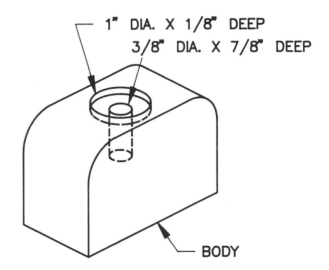

8-22. Drill a 1″ hole to seat the round ball head. Drill a ⅜″ hole for the dowel pin used to attach the head to the shoulder piece.

8-23. Design options for vehicle mailbox drivers. *Left to right:* two 2 × 4 people and one driver with a wood ball head and felt hat.

8-24. Remove wheels, fenders, body, and other parts from the mailbox for painting.

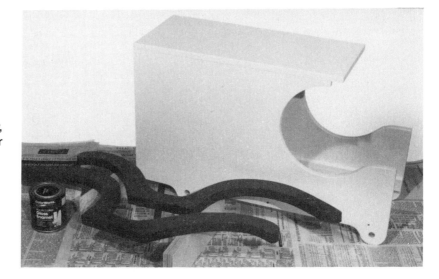

8-25. A piece of ¼″ wide automotive striping tape in a contrasting color is used to decorate this mailbox. Thinner tape can be used to outline doors or windows. (The eagle was painted by hand to customize this project.)

8-26. Full-size eagle pattern for the mail delivery truck.

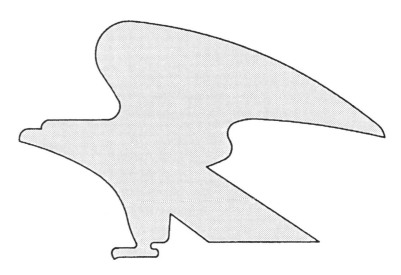

Pickup Truck Mailbox

The overall procedure involved in building the pickup truck (8-1) is almost identical to that of the delivery truck. The pickup truck has several additional pieces, including a seat for mounting the driver, two bed sides, a back, and a bottom piece. These, and all other parts, are identified in the list of materials (Table 8-2). Refer to the plan drawing (8-32) for the sides, and the assembly drawings (8-28–8-31). The relative location of the bed sides, back, and bottom are shown in 8-27. Refer to the instructions and illustrations for the delivery truck.

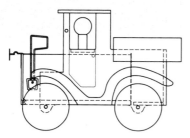

8-27. This illustration shows the relative position of the parts for the pickup truck.

Table 8-2—List of Materials			
(Dimensions are for a #1 or T1 rural mailbox)			
Quantity	Ref. #	Part	Size of Material
1	1	Baseboard	*¾ × 6⅛ × 17½
2	2	Side spacers	½ × 1 × 15½
2	3	Sides	½ × 16⅞ × 21½
2	4	Fenders	¾ × 6⅜ × 24¼
1	5	Roof	½ × 8 × 9
2	6	Bed sides	¾ × 4 × 11½
1	7	Back	½ × 7 × 9⅜
1	8	Bottom	½ × 5 × 7
1	9	Dowel	½ dia. × 8
1	10	Seat	½ × 4 × 7
1	11	Driver body	1½ × 2½ × 3½
1	12	Head	3 dia. wood ball
2	13	Axles	½ dia. × 12
4	14	Axle caps	½ push nut
4	15	Plastic wheels	8 dia.
22	16	Wood screws	1¼ × #8
1	17	Mailbox	Size #1 or T1

*Size of baseboard may vary, depending on the brand of mailbox.

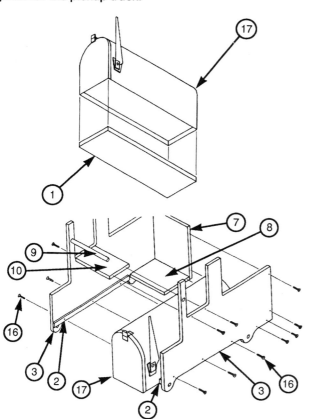

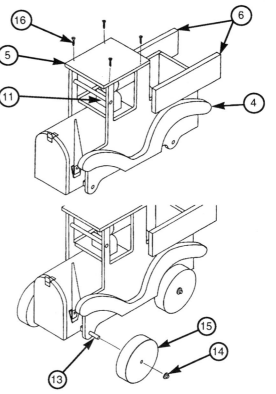

8-28–8-31. Assembly drawings for the pickup truck.

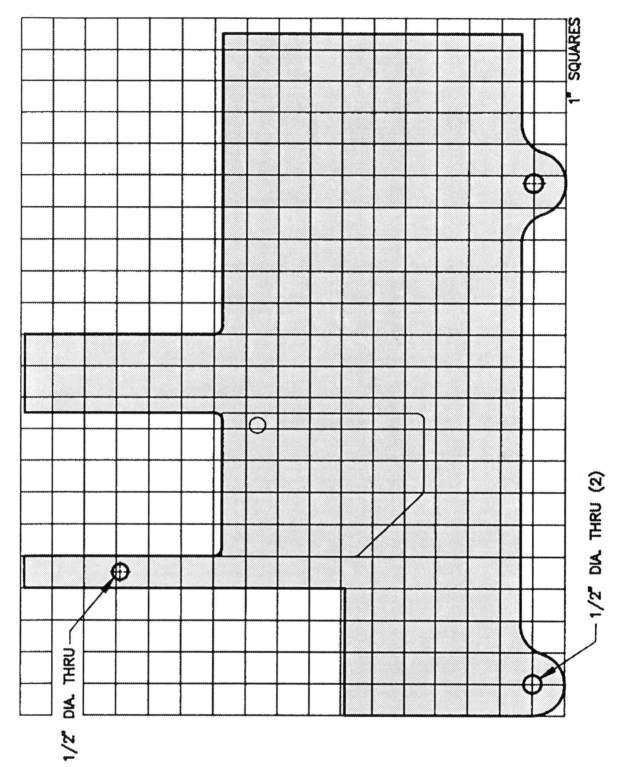

1" SQUARES

1/2" DIA. THRU

1/2" DIA. THRU (2)

1/2" DIA. THRU

8-32. Pickup truck side.

77

Fire Truck Mailbox

The procedure for building the fire truck (8-2) is nearly identical to that of the delivery truck. See 8-38 for the side plan. The fire truck has some additional parts, including a siren, ladders, and a seat for the driver. These parts are all identified in the list of materials (Table 8-3), and the assembly drawings (8-34–8-37). For the relative location of the parts, see 8-33. Refer to the instructions and assembly illustrations for the delivery truck.

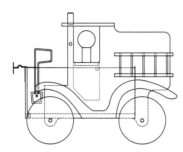

8-33. This illustration shows the relative position of the parts for the fire truck.

Table 8-3—List of Materials
(Dimensions are for a #1 or T1 rural mailbox)

Quantity	Ref. #	Part	Size of Material
1	1	Baseboard	*¾ × 6⅛ × 17½
2	2	Side spacers	½ × 1 × 15½
2	3	Sides	½ × 16⅞ × 21½
2	4	Fenders	¾ × 6⅜ × 24¼
1	5	Roof	½ × 8 × 9
1	6	Siren	1″ dia. × 2
4	7	Ladder rails	½ × ½ × 10
10	8	Ladder rungs	¼ dia. × 4
1	9	Dowel	½ dia. × 8
1	10	Seat	½ × 4 × 7
1	11	Driver body	1½ × 2½ × 3½
1	12	Head	3 dia. wood ball
2	13	Axles	½ dia. × 12
4	14	Axle caps	½ push nut
4	15	Plastic wheels	8 dia.
Misc.	16	Screws	As needed
1	17	Mailbox	Size #1 or T1

*Size of baseboard may vary, depending on the brand of mailbox.

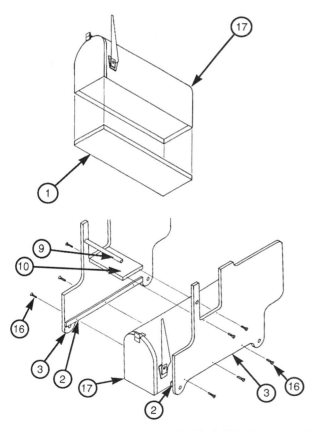

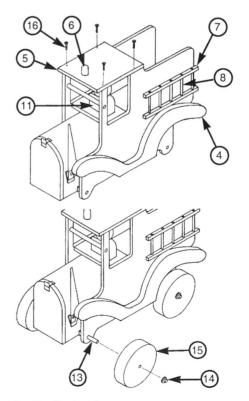

8-34–8-37. Assembly drawings for the fire truck.

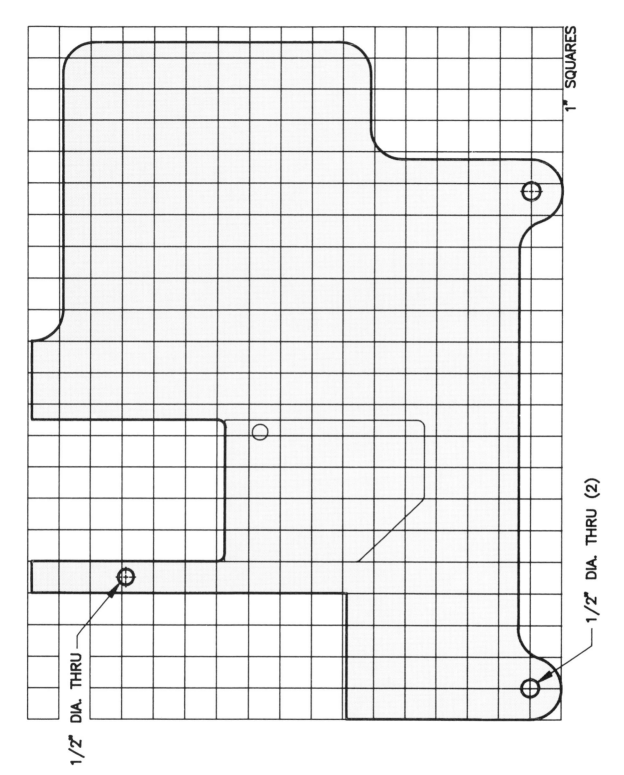

1" SQUARES

1/2" DIA. THRU

1/2" DIA. THRU (2)

8-38. Fire truck side.

Car with Rumble Seat Mailbox

The car mailbox (8-3) is the last design that involves nearly the same construction procedures that are used to make the other vehicles in this chapter. The plan for the side pieces is shown in 8-44. The car also has some of its own special parts, including a crossbar, back, bottom, dowel, and driver's seat. These are all identified in the list of materials (Table 8-4). The assembly is shown in 8-40−8-43.

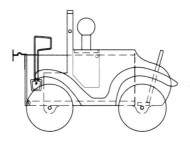

8-39. This illustration shows the relative position of the parts for the car with rumble seat.

Table 8-4—List of Materials
(Dimensions are for a #1 or T1 rural mailbox)

Quantity	Ref. #	Part	Size of Material
1	1	Baseboard	*$\frac{3}{4} \times 6\frac{1}{8} \times 17\frac{1}{2}$
2	2	Side spacers	$\frac{1}{2} \times 1 \times 15\frac{1}{2}$
2	3	Sides	$\frac{1}{2} \times 16\frac{7}{8} \times 21\frac{1}{2}$
2	4	Fenders	$\frac{3}{4} \times 6\frac{3}{8} \times 24\frac{1}{4}$
1	5	Crossbar	$\frac{1}{2} \times 1 \times 8$
1	6	Back	$\frac{1}{2} \times 7 \times 9$
1	7	Bottom	$\frac{1}{2} \times 2 \times 7$
1	8	Dowel	$\frac{1}{2}$ dia. $\times 8$
1	9	Seat	$\frac{1}{2} \times 4 \times 7$
1	10	Driver body	$1\frac{1}{2} \times 2\frac{1}{2} \times 3\frac{1}{2}$
1	11	Head	3 dia. wood ball
2	12	Axles	$\frac{1}{2}$ dia. $\times 12$
4	13	Axle caps	$\frac{1}{2}$ push nut
4	14	Plastic wheels	8 dia.
Misc.	15	Wood screws	As needed
1	16	Mailbox	Size #1 or T1

*Size of baseboard may vary, depending on the brand of mailbox.

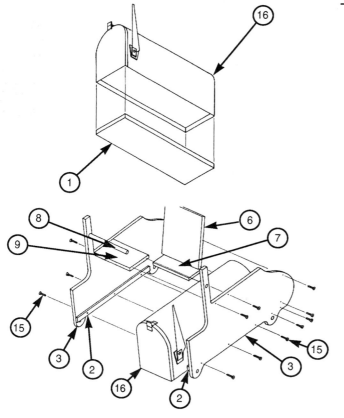

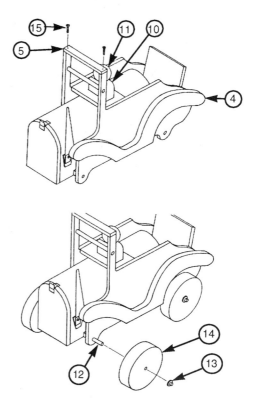

8-40−8-43. Assembly drawings for the car with rumble seat.

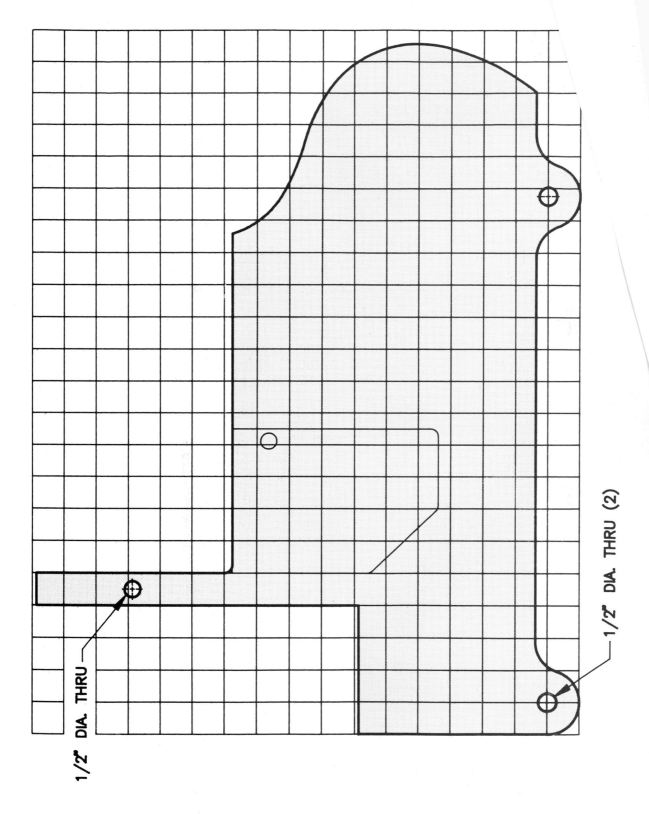

1/2" DIA. THRU

1/2" DIA. THRU (2)

8-44. Car with rum...

9

Tractor

Tractors have changed the lives of farmers dramatically over the past 50 years. Before the invention of the tractor, one-third of Americans worked as farmers. They struggled to raise enough food for the country, because their work was done by hand. Now only two percent of Americans are farmers, but they produce enough food for the entire country.

Since the tractor is the workhorse of the modern farm, it seems a fitting calling card for rural mailboxes across the countryside. This tractor mailbox (9-1) is a symbol of rural America. It is a celebration of the farmer and rural life.

This mailbox involves techniques similar to those of the four vehicles described in Chapter 8. Refer to that information and study drawings 9-2–9-7. Table 9-1 lists all materials required.

Tractor Wheels

Before cutting any stock to size, make or purchase the wheels for this project. It is necessary first to know the axle-hole diameter to make the axle block and to drill the lower holes in the side pieces. The front needs two 6″ diameter wheels, and the back, two 10″ diameter wheels. See Chapter 8 for information on making or purchasing wheels. We used ½″ diameter axles, so the plans are scaled accordingly. Also, the length of the axle will depend on the thickness of the wheels. (Thicker wheels require longer axles.)

Baseboard and Axle Block

Baseboard. Cut the baseboard to fit the recess underneath the mailbox. Set the baseboard aside.

Axle Block. Cut the axle block 1½″ wide × 1½″ thick. (Ref. #8, Table 9-1 and Illus. 9-2.) Cut a ½ ×

½″ groove into the center of one side for the axle. (For a smaller axle, cut the groove accordingly.) For safety, groove a longer length before sawing the stock to the finished 6⅛″ length.

Attach the axle block to the baseboard with the groove upward against the baseboard, and located approximately 3″ from one end of the baseboard. Secure the axle block to the baseboard with screws. Set the assembly aside.

Side Spacers and Sides

Side Spacers. Cut two ½″ × 1″ × 7½″ side spacers (Ref. #2, Table 9-1 and Illus. 9-3). These pieces can be ripped and resawed from a piece of ¾″ pine. The purpose of these strips is to space the sides of the vehicle slightly away from the sides of the mailbox to clear the metal flange at the bottom of the box.

Sides. Enlarge the drawing (9-6) and lay out two side pieces on ½″ plywood. Lay out the left and right sides so the best side of the plywood will face the outside of the project. Mark the location of the holes with a scratch awl while laying out the pattern. The upper hole is for the windshield dowel and should be drilled ½″ diameter. The lower hole is for the axle. Drill this hole to fit the axle.

Tip: The axle should slide through the axle hole. If it is too tight, either redrill the hole 1/64″ larger or ream or sand the hole slightly so the axle slides through.

Glue the spacers to the inside of each side piece (9-3). Note that the side spacers should be even with the front and bottom of the side pieces.

With the baseboard removed, clamp the side/side spacer assembly to the side of the mailbox. The bottom of the assembly should be even with the

9-1. The tractor mailbox is the definitive symbol of rural America.

bottom of the mailbox, and the side spacer should be against the lip on the back of the mailbox. Drill two ⁹⁄₆₄″ clearance holes all the way through the side assembly and lower lip of the mailbox.

Before attaching the tractor sides, replace the baseboard in the recess underneath the mailbox (9-2). The axle block end of the baseboard faces the front of the mailbox. The other end of the baseboard should butt against the back of the mailbox. Secure the side pieces with 2¼″ × #6 trim-head drywall screws. These screws will go through the side piece, the spacer, the mailbox lip, and into the baseboard.

Seat, Windshield Dowel, and Driver

Seat. After the tractor sides are attached, check to be sure they are parallel with each other (vertically, and square with the bottom of the mailbox). Measure the total width between the two sides. This will determine the length of the board used for the tractor seat (Ref. #7 in Table 9-1 and Illus. 9-3). Cut the seat to fit the distance between the side pieces.

Table 9-1—List of Materials
(Dimensions are for a #1 or T1 rural mailbox)

Quantity	Ref. #	Part	Size of Material
1	1	Baseboard	*¾ × 6⅛ × 17½
2	2	Spacers	½ × 1 × 7½
2	3	Sides	½ × 10½ × 15½
2	4	Fenders	¾ × 3¾ × 8½
1	5	Roof	½ × 9 × 12
1	6	Windshield dowel	½ dia. × 8
1	7	Seat	½ × 4 × 7
1	8	Axle block	1½ × 1½ × 6⅛
1	9	Driver body	1½ × 2½ × 3
1	10	Head	3 dia. wood ball
1	11	Smokestack	1¼ × 2⅝
2	12	Axles	½ dia. × 12
4	13	Axle caps	½ push nut
2	14	Plastic wheels	6 dia.
2	15	Plastic wheels	10 dia.
Misc.	16	Wood screws	As needed
1	17	Mailbox	Size #1 or T1

*Size of baseboard may vary, depending on the brand of mailbox.

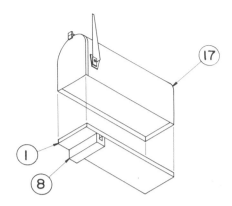

9-2. Axle block and baseboard assembly.

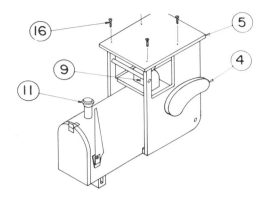

9-4. Installation of driver, smokestack, roof, and fenders.

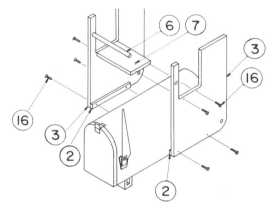

9-3. Exploded assembly of sides, side spacers, seat, and windshield dowel.

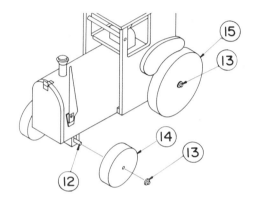

9-5. Installation of wheels.

Windshield Dowel. The windshield dowel (Ref. #6 in Table 9-1 and Illus. 9-3) is cut to the same length as the width of the cab (approximately 8″).

Driver. Before attaching the seat and the dowel, make the driver (see Chapter 8). The height of the driver, including hat, should fit between the seat board and the roof. With wood screws, attach the driver to the seat. Attach the seat to the sides, and glue the windshield dowel in place.

Roof, Fenders, and Smokestack

Roof. Cut the roof (Ref. #5, Table 9-1) from ½″ plywood, and attach with screws. The roof should be 1″ wider than the width of the vehicle, so it extends over each side.

Fenders. Cut the fenders (9-7) from ¾″ stock. Locate the fenders by positioning the inside radius of the fenders approximately ⅝″ from the top of the rear wheels. The fenders extend 1½″ beyond the back edge of the side pieces. Attach the fenders with wood screws (see 9-4).

Smokestack. Turned-wood smokestacks (Ref. #11 in Table 9-1 and Illus. 9-4) are available from most woodworking supply catalogs. Drill a ⁹⁄₆₄″ pilot hole in the bottom of the smokestack. Drill an ¹¹⁄₆₄″ clearance hole on the top of the mailbox, about 4″ from the front. To attach the smokestack, use a 1″ × #8 sheet metal screw installed from the inside of the mailbox.

Finishing Details

Sanding. Remove all wood pieces and finish-sand. Fill any voids with wood putty.

Painting. See Chapter 1 for tips on priming and painting. Choose the colors of your favorite brand tractor. We used green for the mailbox and most wood parts. The smokestack and fenders were painted yellow.

After all parts are dry, reassemble. Touch up the wood screw heads with the appropriate color paint. Install the wheels (9-5).

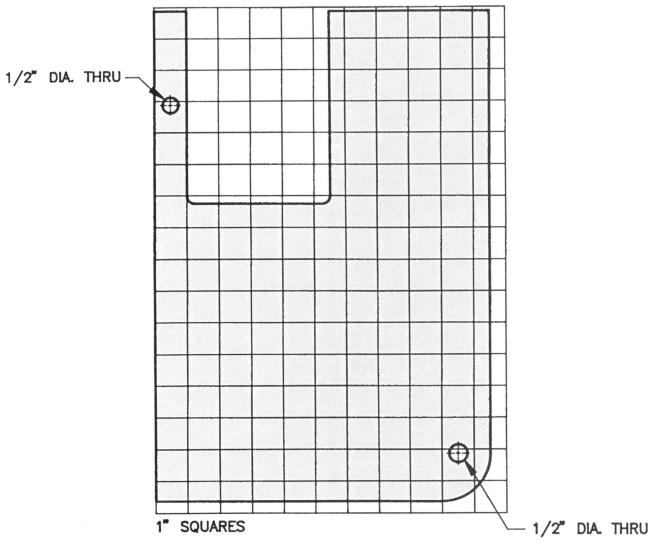

1/2" DIA. THRU

1" SQUARES

1/2" DIA. THRU

9-6. Tractor side.

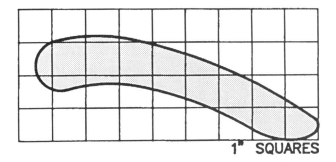

1" SQUARES

9-7. Fenders.

10
Locomotive

Many of us have fond memories of a childhood train ride or playing with a model train set. This old-fashioned steam locomotive is a celebration of those bygone days. It is complete with an engineer in a striped uniform.

Table 10-1 lists all materials required.

Drilling Attachment Holes

Because of the large number of parts that are attached to the mailbox, begin by drilling all the holes specified in 10-2. The $9/64''$ and $11/64''$ holes will have parts attached with #6 and #8 screws, respectively.

Baseboard, Wheels, and Cylinder

Baseboard. Cut out a baseboard to fit the mailbox, but do not install it.

Large Wheels/Wheel Details. Each wheel is made in two layers: one detailed and one a flat disc. The position of the wheels and cylinder is shown in 10-3. Make six large-wheel discs from $1/2''$ stock, and six large wheel details from $1/8''$ or $1/4''$ stock. See 10-4–10-5. All pieces can be made of exterior-grade plywood. The pie-shaped openings in the large-wheel detail pieces can be cut with a scroll saw or simply painted on.

Glue the detailed wheel to the plain-wheel disc with exterior glue and drill the $9/64''$ hole through for each assembly.

Small Wheels/Wheel Details. Make six plain small wheels (10-6) and six small-wheel details (10-7). Drill all holes as specified. Glue the detailed wheels to the flat wheel discs.

Cylinder. The cylinders (10-8) are cut from $1¼''$ diameter dowel. Drill the three holes in the dowel, as specified.

Tip: Be sure to clamp the cylinder securely before drilling the holes in the end grain to prevent the piece from spinning.

Glue a $3/4''$ screw-hole button into the appropriate end of each cylinder.

The Smokestack and Other Parts

Except for the pushrod assembly, these components are all attached to the front and top of the mailbox. For an exploded view, see 10-9.

Smokestack. The smokestack mount (10-10) has a bottom cut to match the curve on the top of the mailbox. Drill the large hole on top to accommodate a wood smokestack. Smokestacks are available from many woodworking supply catalogs.

Steam Domes. The steam domes (10-11) are cut from $1¼''$ dowel rod.

Bell Mount. The bell mount (10-12) is cut from $1/2''$ plywood. The $1/16''$ hole is drilled all the way through for simplicity. The screw eye is installed in this hole to hold the $1''$ metal bell. The top of the hole should be filled with wood filler.

Headlight. The headlight mount (10-13) can be cut from $1/2''$ or $3/4''$ thick stock. *Tip:* Drill the $1''$ diameter hole before sawing the headlight mount to size. This makes it easier to clamp. Cut out and sand the headlight mount and glue the headlight (a $1''$ screw-hole button) in place. Drill a $1/8''$ hole $1/2''$ deep from the back of the headlight assembly.

Cowcatcher. The cowcatcher (10-14) must be glued from several pieces of flat, solid stock. Glue

10-1. Locomotive mailbox.

Table 10-1—List of Materials
(Dimensions are for a #1 or T1 rural mailbox)

Quantity	Part	Size of Material	Quantity	Part	Size of Material
1	Baseboard	*³⁄₄ × 6⅛ × 17½	1	Cab center	½ × 6½ × 7¼
4	Small wheel	½ × 2 dia.	1	Cab roof	½ × 9¼ × 9½
4	Small-wheel detail	⅛ × 1¾ dia.	1	Engineer	1½ × 2½ × 3½
6	Large wheel	½ × 4¼ dia.	2	Arm (engineer)	⅜ × ½ × 1⅝
6	Large-wheel detail	⅛ × 3⅞ dia.	1	Hat brim (engineer)	⅛ × 1¼ × 2
2	Cylinder	1¼ dia. × 3¼	1	Hat (engineer)	1¼ dia. × ⅞
1	Smokestack mount	1⅛ × 1½ × 1½	13	Sheet metal screw	½ × #8
2	Steam dome	1¼ dia. × 1⅜	10	Trim-head drywall screw	1⅝ × #6
1	Bell mount	½ × 2¾ × 3¼	6	Drywall screw	1¼ × #6
1	Headlight mount	½ × 1½ × 1½	1	Screw eye	¹³⁄₁₆ × ⁹⁄₃₂ dia.
1	Cowcatcher	2¾ × 3⁵⁄₁₆ × 6	1	Round bell	1 dia.
6	Pushrod block	⅝ × ⅝ × 1¼	1	Large smokestack	1¾ × 3¼
2	Pushrod	⁷⁄₁₆ dia. × 13¹⁵⁄₁₆	2	Screw-hole button	¾ dia.
2	Cab side	½ × 7½ × 11	1	Screw-hole button	1 dia.
2	Cab front/back	½ × 5½ × 7¼	1	Black-mailbox	Size #1 or T1

Exterior enamel paint recommendations: white, red, light blue, dark blue, black.

*Size of baseboard may vary, depending on the brand of mailbox.

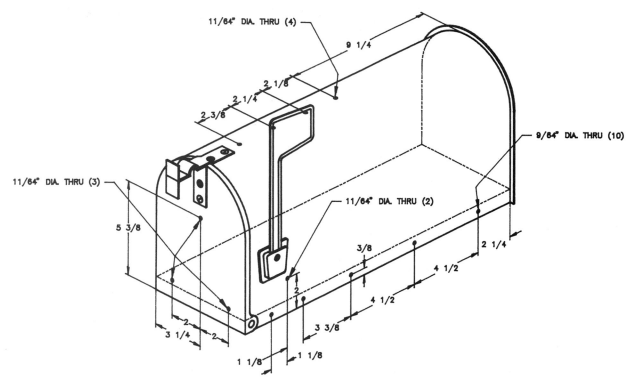

10-2. Predrill holes in the steel mailbox, as shown.

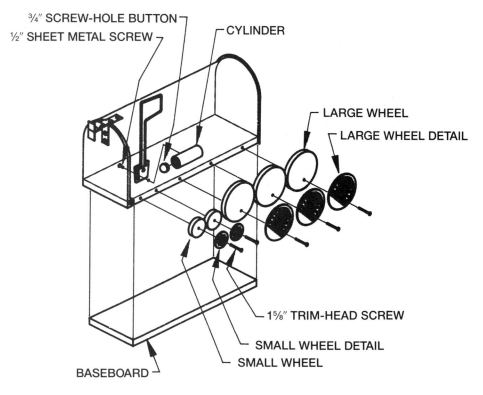

10-3. This exploded assembly drawing shows the installation of the wheels and cylinder.

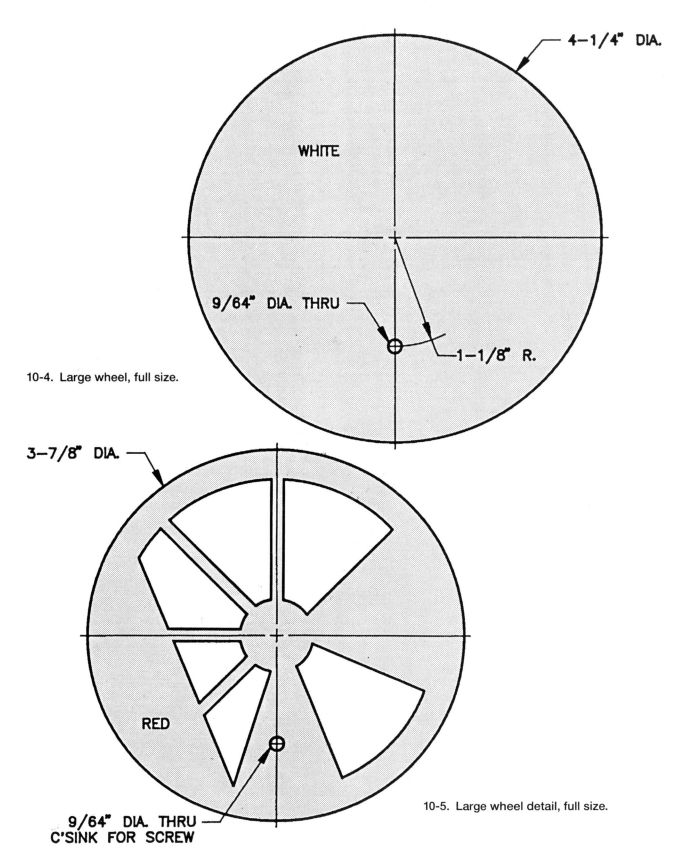

4–1/4" DIA.

WHITE

9/64" DIA. THRU

1–1/8" R.

10-4. Large wheel, full size.

3–7/8" DIA.

RED

10-5. Large wheel detail, full size.

9/64" DIA. THRU
C'SINK FOR SCREW

89

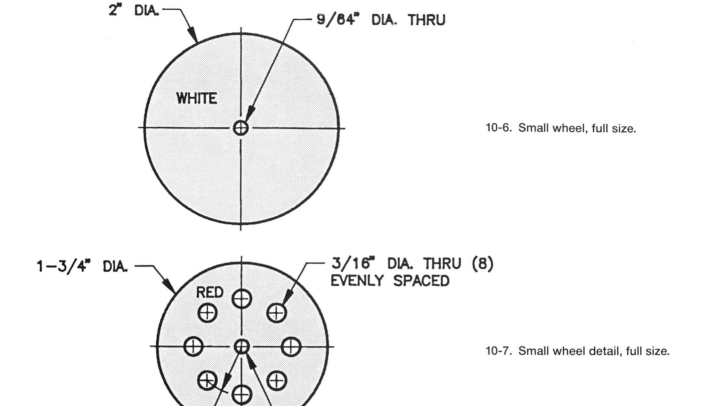

2" DIA.

9/64" DIA. THRU

WHITE

10-6. Small wheel, full size.

1–3/4" DIA.

3/16" DIA. THRU (8)
EVENLY SPACED

RED

10-7. Small wheel detail, full size.

1/2" R.

9/64" DIA. THRU
C'SINK FOR SCREW

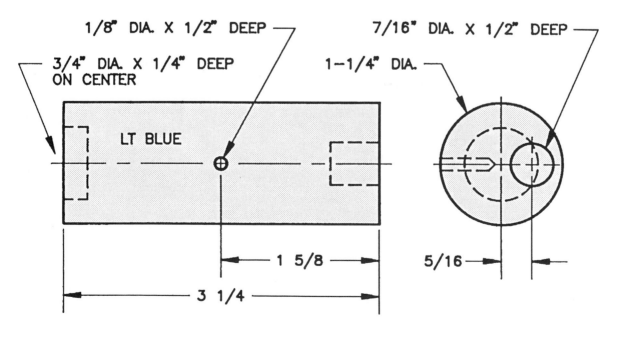

1/8" DIA. X 1/2" DEEP

7/16" DIA. X 1/2" DEEP

3/4" DIA. X 1/4" DEEP
ON CENTER

1–1/4" DIA.

LT BLUE

1 5/8

5/16

3 1/4

10-8. Cylinder, side- and end-view details.

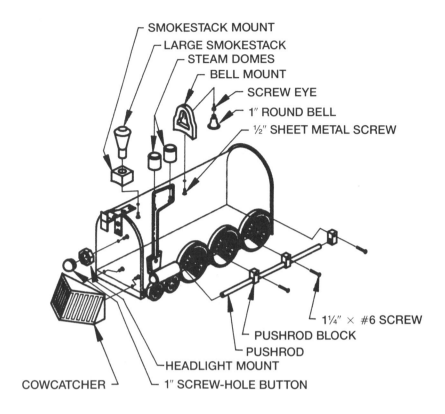

SMOKESTACK MOUNT
LARGE SMOKESTACK
STEAM DOMES
BELL MOUNT
SCREW EYE
1″ ROUND BELL
½″ SHEET METAL SCREW

1¼″ × #6 SCREW
PUSHROD BLOCK
PUSHROD
HEADLIGHT MOUNT
1″ SCREW-HOLE BUTTON
COWCATCHER

10-9. This exploded assembly drawing shows the positions of the accessories that mount to the front and top of the mailbox, as well as the pushrod assembly.

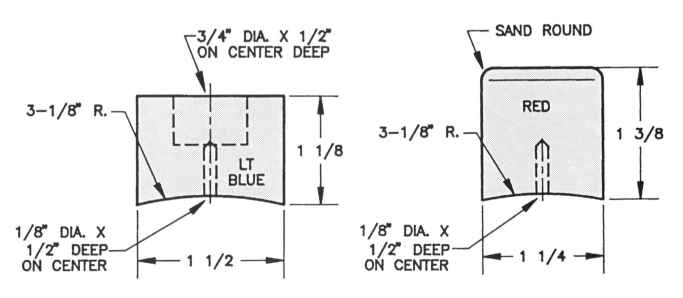

3/4″ DIA. X 1/2″ ON CENTER DEEP

3-1/8″ R.

1 1/8

LT BLUE

1/8″ DIA. X 1/2″ DEEP ON CENTER

1 1/2

10-10. Smokestack mount detail.

SAND ROUND

RED

3-1/8″ R.

1 3/8

1/8″ DIA. X 1/2″ DEEP ON CENTER

1 1/4

10-11. Steam dome detail.

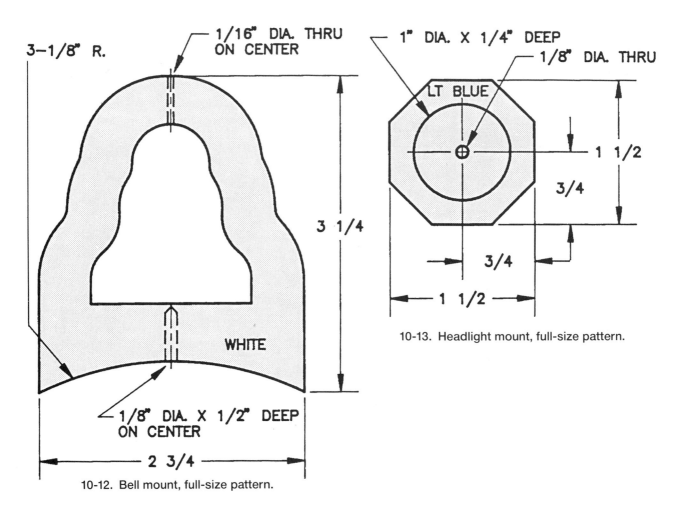

3–1/8" R.

1/16" DIA. THRU
ON CENTER

1" DIA. X 1/4" DEEP

1/8" DIA. THRU

LT BLUE

1 1/2

3/4

3/4

1 1/2

3 1/4

WHITE

1/8" DIA. X 1/2" DEEP
ON CENTER

2 3/4

10-13. Headlight mount, full-size pattern.

10-12. Bell mount, full-size pattern.

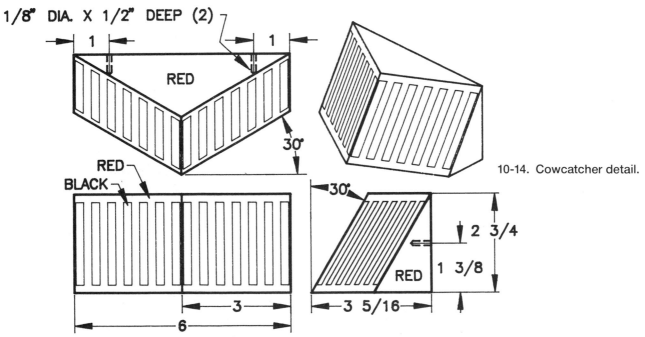

1/8" DIA. X 1/2" DEEP (2)

1

1

RED

30°

RED

BLACK

30°

2 3/4

1 3/8

RED

3 5/16

3

6

10-14. Cowcatcher detail.

92

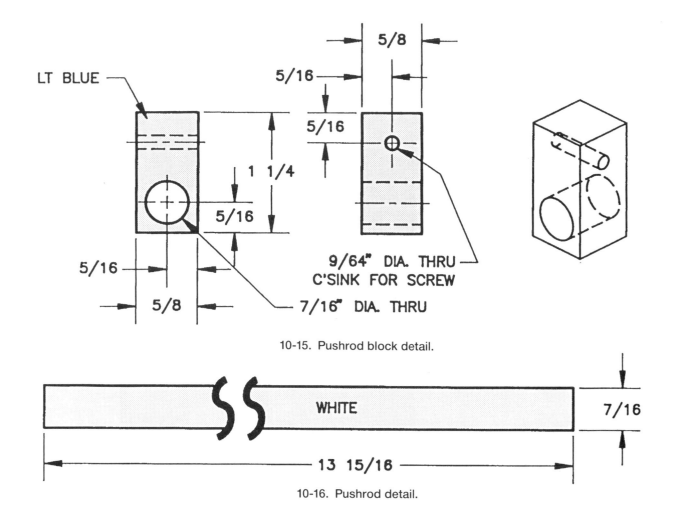

LT BLUE

5/8

5/16

5/16

1 1/4

5/16

5/16

5/8

9/64" DIA. THRU
C'SINK FOR SCREW

7/16" DIA. THRU

10-15. Pushrod block detail.

WHITE

7/16

13 15/16

10-16. Pushrod detail.

6"-wide boards, which are about 12" long, to get a block 2¾" thick by 6" wide by 12" long. Although the length of this piece is only 3⁵⁄₁₆", the extra length makes machining easier and safer, because there is more wood to hold on to when sawing the compound angles required to shape the front. These angles can be cut using a table saw or by carefully measuring and then sawing with a hand saw. Another advantage of starting with a longer piece is that if the first angle cuts do not meet exactly in the center, enough material remains to try again. After the compound angles are cut on one end of the glue-up, cross-cut off the cowcatcher at a length of 3⁵⁄₁₆".

Pushrod Assembly. Cut six pushrod blocks (10-15) and two pushrods (10-16). *Tip:* Because wood

10-17 *Right:* Exploded assembly drawing showing the installation of the cab and engineer. The cab is assembled and fastened to the mailbox with four ½" sheet metal screws, driven from the inside outward.

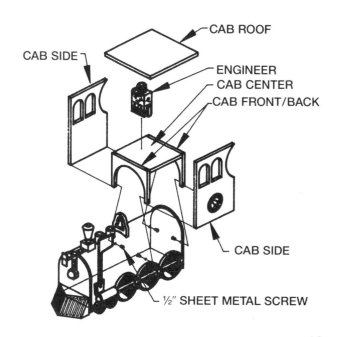

CAB ROOF

CAB SIDE

ENGINEER
CAB CENTER
CAB FRONT/BACK

CAB SIDE

½" SHEET METAL SCREW

dowels often run slightly oversize, you may have to drill the ⁷⁄₁₆″ diameter hole slightly larger (²⁹⁄₆₄″). Note that this hole and the ⁹⁄₆₄″ holes are both drilled all the way through the pushrod blocks.

Cab and Engineer

Cab. See the exploded assembly drawing (10-17). Cut the cab sides (10-18), cab front and back (10-19), cab center and cab roof (10-20) from ½″ plywood. Finish-sand and assemble the cab with glue and nails or screws.

Engineer. The train engineer shown in 10-21 is based on the 2 × 4 style driver discussed and illustrated in Chapter 8. The only difference is the addition of the hat and the stripes.

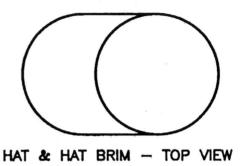

HAT & HAT BRIM — TOP VIEW

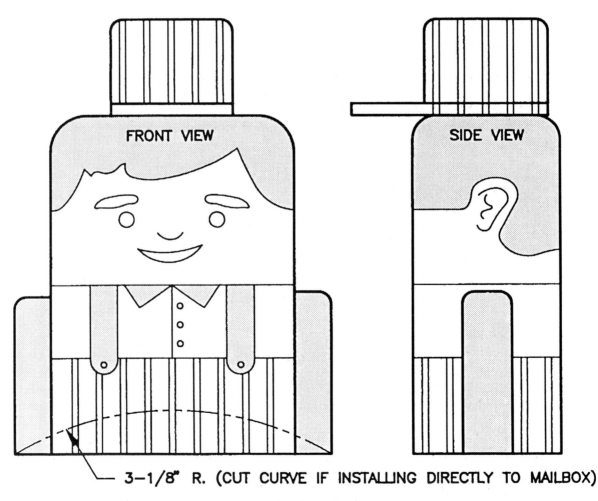

FRONT VIEW

SIDE VIEW

3–1/8″ R. (CUT CURVE IF INSTALLING DIRECTLY TO MAILBOX)

10-21. Engineer detail.

Cut the body and two arms according to the dimensions in Table 10-1. To make the hat top, cut a ⅞" length of 1¼" diameter dowel stock. The hat brim can be cut from ⅛" or ¼" plywood. Glue the hat assembly in place. Drill screw-mounting holes as required in the cab center piece and in the bottom of the engineer.

Final Assembly

Install the baseboard and wheels with 1⅝" × #6 trim-head drywall screws (10-3). Attach each cylinder with a sheet metal screw driven from the inside of the mailbox (10-3) with the mailbox on its side. Slide the pushrod in the end of the cylinder and slide all three pushrod blocks onto the pushrod. Position the rear pushrod block flush with the end of the pushrod, and drill a ⁷⁄₆₄" pilot hole through the small hole in the pushrod block and into the rear train wheel. (Be sure the pushrod is horizontal.) Temporarily secure it with a 1¼ × #6 wood screw. Drill the pilot holes for the other two blocks, making sure they are located in the same relative position on their respective train wheels. Glue the pushrod in the blocks and secure the assembly with wood screws.

Install all accessories to the top and front with #8 sheet metal screws. Install the engineer to the cab center. Install the completed cab to the back of the mailbox using sheet metal screws (10-17).

Finishing

Finish-sand all wood pieces and prime and paint them. You may wish to choose colors that represent railroads of significance to you or to your geographical area. The colors we chose were based on a color picture of an old Great Northern railroad engine.

Decals (10-22) applied to the sides give the project the perfect final touch. The decals are manufactured by Virnex Industries and can be ordered from the Walthers World of N & Z Scale catalog, part #762-102. The Walthers catalog is available in almost every hobby shop that carries model trains. This catalog lists decals for over 60 different railroads.

The stripes on the engineer were done with ¹⁄₁₆" wide automotive striping tape. The stripes on the cowcatcher were done with ³⁄₁₆" wide automotive striping tape.

A black prepainted steel mailbox was used for this project.

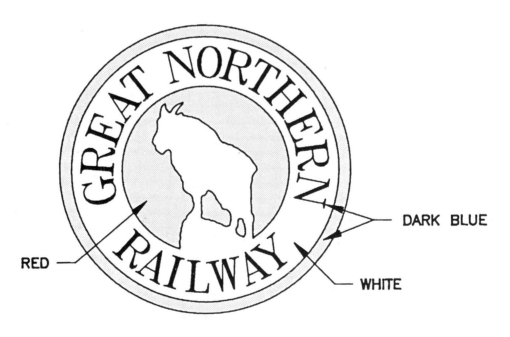

RED

DARK BLUE

WHITE

10-22. One of 60 railroad logo decals available.

11

Single-Wing Airplane

This mailbox was designed with airplane enthusiasts in mind. It turns out people from all walks of life enjoy the design, simply because it's adorable and fits the "air mail" theme. If you really want to make a statement, you could place the postal-delivery-truck mailbox (see Chapter 8) at the standard height for your mail and the airplane mailbox about 10 feet higher for "air mail" delivery.

One unique design feature is that the propellers really turn in the wind. This is very eye-catching and gives life to the finished project.

Table 11-1 lists all materials required.

Baseboard and Wing

Baseboard. Cut the baseboard to fit the recess underneath the mailbox. Set it aside for later use.

Wing. Cut the wing (11-2) to size from ½" plywood. Note that the center portion of the wing is narrower by 2" than the rest of the wing. This is to prevent interference when mounted to the post. This extra cut may not be necessary; it depends on how the mailbox will be mounted.

The wing is attached to the baseboard approximately 2" from the front end of the mailbox. See 11-3. Fasten with 1¼" screws. With the wing attached, fasten the baseboard to the metal box with three sheet metal screws on each side.

Pilot Head and Rudder

Pilot. The simplest way to create the pilot is to screw a 3" diameter wooden ball to the top of the mailbox, 9" from the front (11-4).

An optional set of shoulders for the pilot is shown in 11-5. The shoulders are cut from a piece of 2 × 4"

stock, and the radius is cut on the bottom of the block to fit around the top curve of the mailbox. The head is secured to the shoulders with a ⅜" dowel pin. This pilot is similar to the mailbox vehicle drivers described in Chapter 8, except he has been painted with a brown "leather" flying helmet and goggles. Doll sunglasses can also be used.

Rudder (11-6). Cut the rudder from ½" plywood. Sand and attach it to the back of the mailbox with two 1 × #8 hex-head sheet metal screws. This piece should be centered on the back of the mailbox as close to the top as possible.

Nacelles, Elevator, Propellers

Nacelles (motor parts). Cut two large nacelles (11-7) and four small nacelles (11-8) from ¾" stock. Finish-sand and glue the nacelle assemblies together. Be sure the flat sides in the front and bottom are all even. See 11-9. Attach the nacelles to the wing so they are centered at a point 8" from the tip of the wing. The nacelles must be even with the front of the wing so the propellers will spin freely.

Elevator. Cut the elevator (11-11). The ½" slot in the elevator cross-laps with the ½" slot in the rudder. Finish-sand and glue the elevator in the slot, as shown in 11-9.

Propellers. Cut two propellers (11-12) from pine or redwood stock (¾" × 1" × 8"). The propeller blades can be cut on a band saw using the procedure shown in 11-13, steps one through eight. Or, carve them with a good whittling knife.

Note: The instructions show how to lay out propellers that will spin in opposite directions. The completed propellers are attached to the nacelles

11-1. The amusing single-wing airplane with pilot.

with 2 × #6 round head wood screws (11-10). The center hole of the propeller can be drilled slightly larger to accommodate a small nylon or brass bushing.

Finishing

Painting. Remove all pieces from the mailbox for painting. General painting suggestions are given in Chapter 1. Painting outlines for the pilot are shown in 11-5. The "leather" flying helmet is painted brown. The goggles can be painted, as shown in the illustration, or use miniature sunglasses, as shown in the color photo section, which follows page 32. These glasses are available at craft shops.

Table 11-1—List of Materials
(Dimensions are for a #1 or T1 rural mailbox)

Quantity	Ref. #	Part	Size of Material
1	1	Baseboard	*¾ × 6⅛ × 17½
1	2	Wing	½ × 7 × 32
2	3	Propellers	¾ × 1 × 8
2	4	Large nacelles	¾ × 2½ × 5
4	5	Small nacelles	¾ × 2 × 5
1	6	Rudder	¾ × 4½ × 7¾
1	7	Elevator	½ × 4 × 11½
1	8	Pilot head	3 dia. wood ball
2	9	Wood screw	1¼ × #8
2	10	Rd. hd. wood screw	2 × #6
4	11	Washer	3/16 I.D.
1		Hex-hd. sheet metal screw	1 × #8
1	12	Mailbox	Size #1 or T1

Exterior enamel paint recommendations: red, yellow, brown, black, beige.

*Size of baseboard may vary, depending on the brand of mailbox.

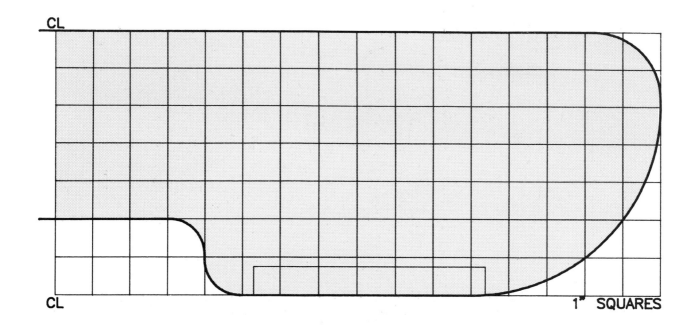

CL

CL

1" SQUARES

11-2. Wing, half plan.

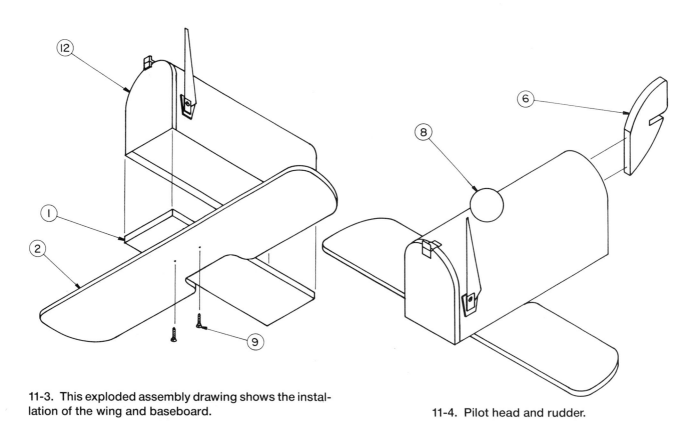

11-3. This exploded assembly drawing shows the installation of the wing and baseboard.

11-4. Pilot head and rudder.

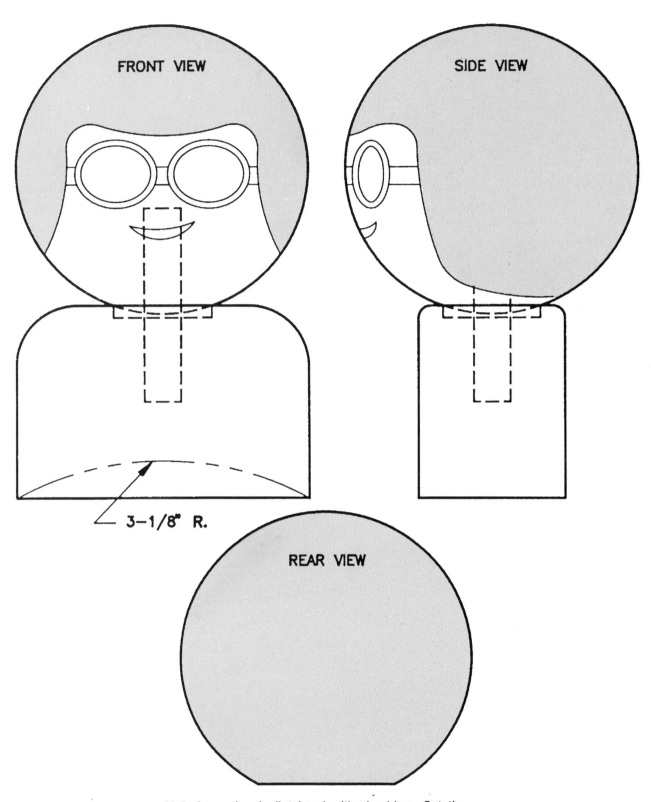

FRONT VIEW

SIDE VIEW

3-1/8" R.

REAR VIEW

11-5. An optional pilot head with shoulders. Cut the body 1½ × 2 × 3". Attach the body and head with a ⅜" diameter dowel pin that is 2" long.

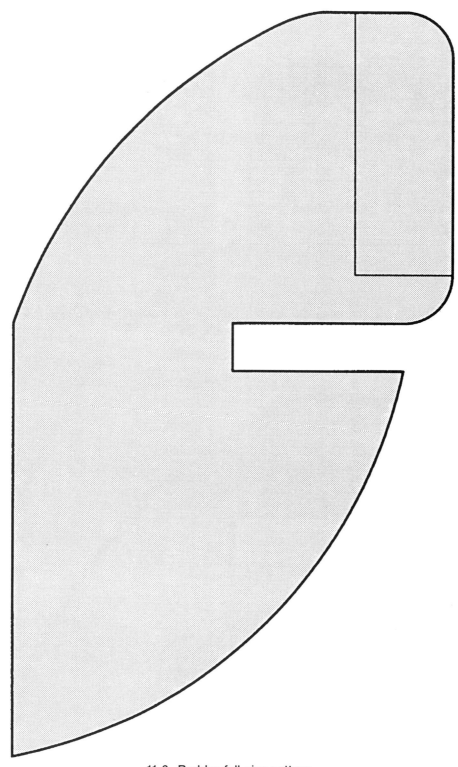

11-6. Rudder, full-size pattern.

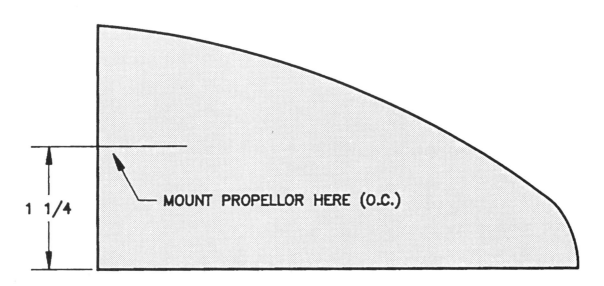

1 1/4

MOUNT PROPELLOR HERE (O.C.)

11-7. Large nacelles, full-size pattern.

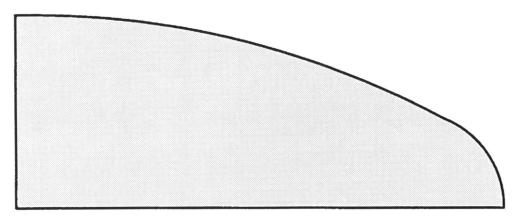

11-8. Small nacelles, full-size pattern.

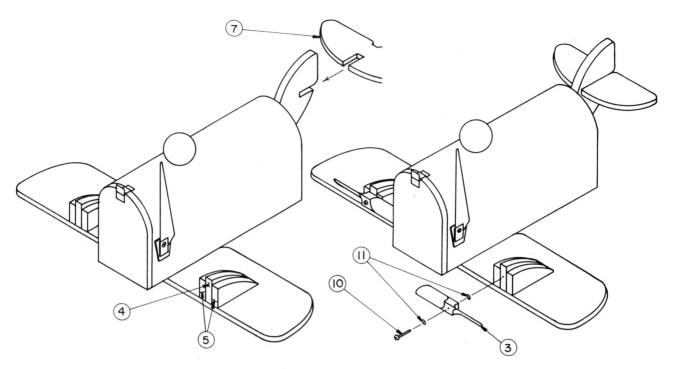

11-9. This drawing shows assembly of the elevator and nacelles.

11-10. Installation of the propellers.

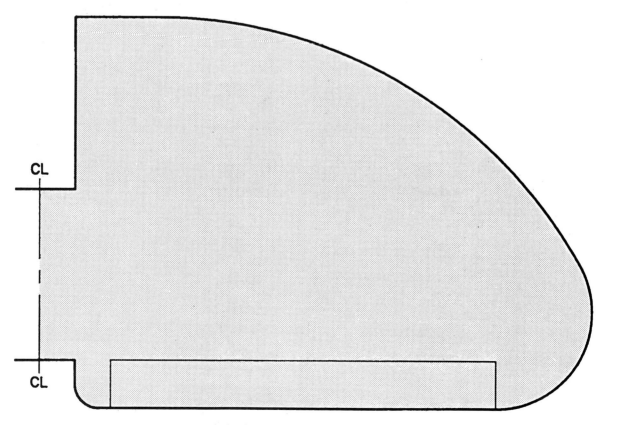

CL

CL

11-11. Elevator, full-size pattern. Flip pattern over for other half.

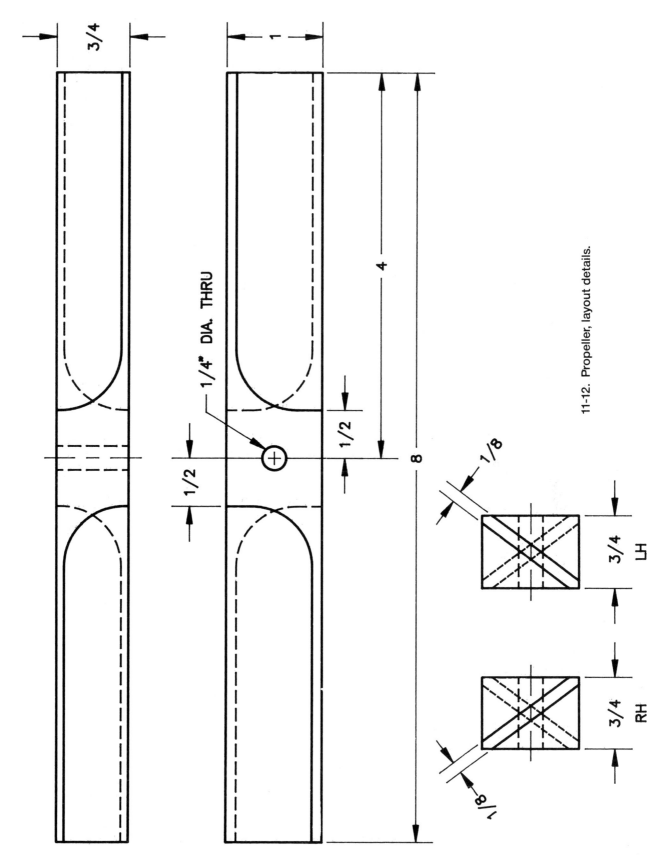

3/4

1

1/4" DIA. THRU

4

1/2

1/2

8

1/8

3/4

LH

3/4

RH

1/8

11-12. Propeller, layout details.

105

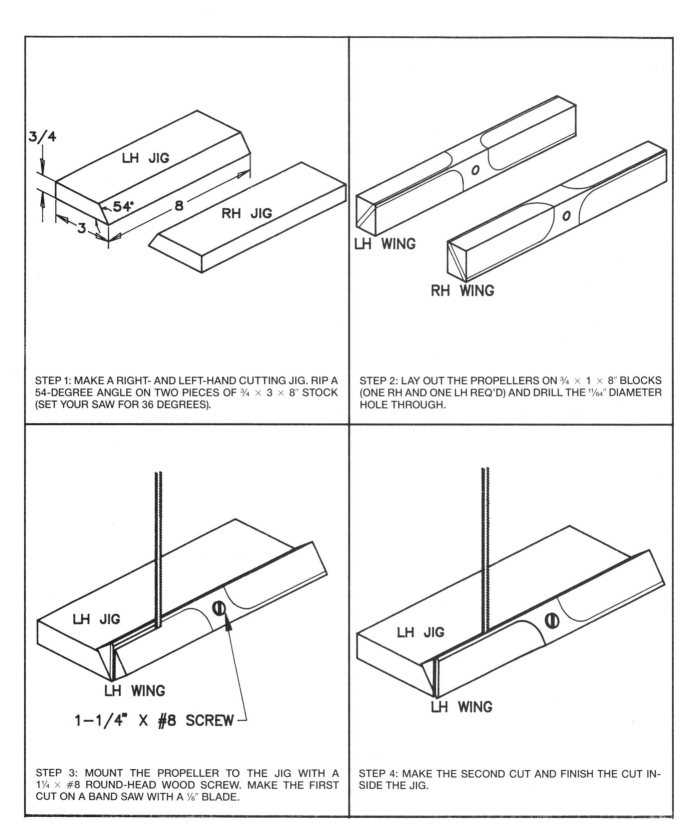

STEP 1: MAKE A RIGHT- AND LEFT-HAND CUTTING JIG. RIP A 54-DEGREE ANGLE ON TWO PIECES OF ¾ × 3 × 8″ STOCK (SET YOUR SAW FOR 36 DEGREES).

STEP 2: LAY OUT THE PROPELLERS ON ¾ × 1 × 8″ BLOCKS (ONE RH AND ONE LH REQ'D) AND DRILL THE ¹¹⁄₆₄″ DIAMETER HOLE THROUGH.

STEP 3: MOUNT THE PROPELLER TO THE JIG WITH A 1¼ × #8 ROUND-HEAD WOOD SCREW. MAKE THE FIRST CUT ON A BAND SAW WITH A ⅛″ BLADE.

STEP 4: MAKE THE SECOND CUT AND FINISH THE CUT IN-SIDE THE JIG.

11-13. These eight steps describe how to make and use a special jig to cut left- and right-hand rotating propellers, using a band saw.

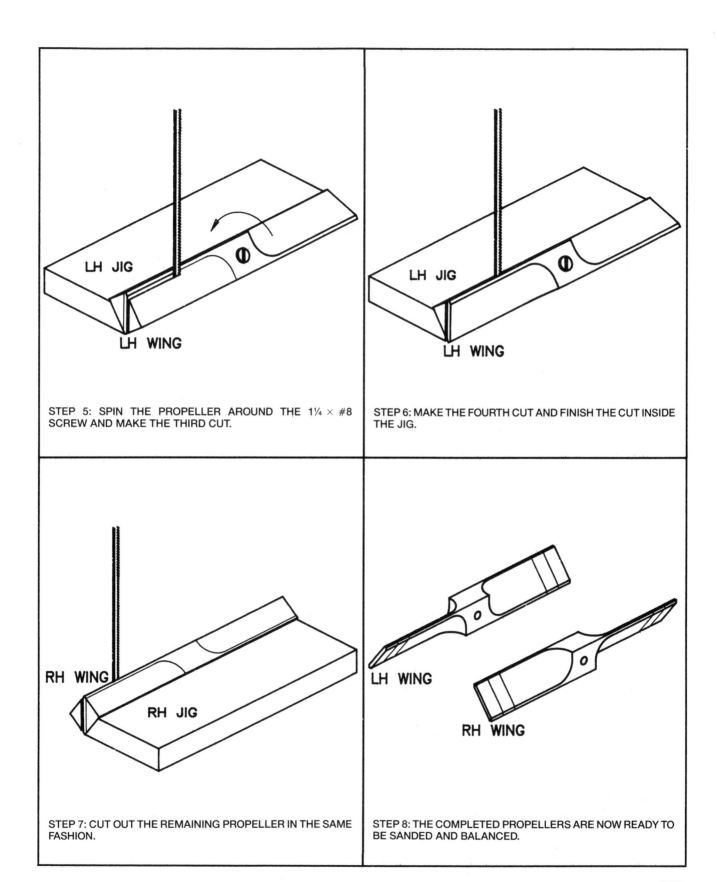

STEP 5: SPIN THE PROPELLER AROUND THE 1¼ × #8 SCREW AND MAKE THE THIRD CUT.

STEP 6: MAKE THE FOURTH CUT AND FINISH THE CUT INSIDE THE JIG.

STEP 7: CUT OUT THE REMAINING PROPELLER IN THE SAME FASHION.

STEP 8: THE COMPLETED PROPELLERS ARE NOW READY TO BE SANDED AND BALANCED.

12
Triwing Airplane

The Red Baron was probably the best-known fighter pilot in World War I. This German aviator, Baron Manfred von Richthofen, was shot down and killed by a Canadian pilot over France in 1918. The Baron's reputation for shooting down Allied airplanes from his red Fokker triplane is legendary.

This triplane mailbox can be equipped humorously with a Holstein cow pilot, or use a round-ball-head pilot, such as those illustrated in Chapter 11.

Table 12-1 lists all the materials required.

Baseboard and Tail Assembly

Baseboard. Cut the baseboard to fit the recess underneath the mailbox. Attach the baseboard with small sheet metal screws. See the exploded assembly drawing, 12-2.

Lay out the tail spacer, elevator, and rudder patterns onto ½″ stock and cut out. See 12-2–12-5. Drill the holes specified, and finish-sand all pieces.

Position the tail spacer on the back of the mailbox, and use it as a drilling guide to drill the three ¹¹⁄₆₄″ holes through the rear of the metal mailbox.

Attach the tail spacer, elevator, and rudder to the mailbox with three 2″ × #8 sheet metal screws. Fasten them from the inside of the mailbox with the screws extending through the back of the box, through the tail spacer, and into the elevator and rudder (12-2).

Cow Pilot, Cleats

Cow Pilot. Lay out the cow-pilot pattern onto ½″ stock and cut out (12-6). Drill the two ⁹⁄₆₄″ holes specified on the pattern. Finish-sand.

Cleats. Lay out and cut two cleats from ¾″ stock. The cleats are located inside the box and are used to

anchor the cow pilot with screws driven through the top of the mailbox. Instructions for making and installing cleats are given on page 19. Drill a ¹¹⁄₆₄″ diameter hole vertically through each cleat on center. Locate the position of the cow pilot directly on top of the mailbox (on center) and 4¾″ back from the front of the mailbox. See 12-7.

Use the two holes drilled in the bottom of the cow pilot as a layout guide. Mark and drill two ¹¹⁄₆₄″ diameter holes through the top of the mailbox. Attach the pilot to the mailbox with 2″ sheet metal screws. After this initial fitting, remove the pilot and set aside.

Bottom Wing and Landing Gear

Lay out the bottom wing, the landing gear, and the landing-gear wing patterns onto ½″ stock and cut out. See 12-8–12-11. Note that slightly more than half the bottom wing is shown on the grid pattern (12-9). Since the wing is symmetrical, the area to the left of the center line (CL) is identical to the area to the right of the center line. The complete wing should measure 4⅜″ × 23¼″. Drill all holes in these pieces, except the ½″ diameter holes in the wing. These ½″ holes will be drilled in a later step. Finish-sand all parts.

Assemble the bottom wing, landing-gear wing, and landing gear with 1″ × #8 flat-head wood screws, as shown in 12-8. Do not attach the axle pegs and wheels until the pieces have been painted. After this initial fitting, remove the landing-gear assembly from the lower wing and set it aside.

Top Wing and Center Wings

Lay out the top and center wings onto ½″ stock (12-12–12-13). Note that a notch for the flag is cut

12-1. The famous Red Baron's Fokker Triplane can be piloted by this humorous cow or by pilots of other designs.

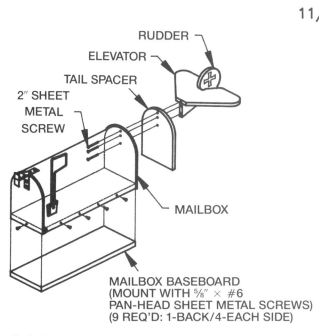

RUDDER

ELEVATOR

TAIL SPACER

2″ SHEET
METAL
SCREW

MAILBOX

MAILBOX BASEBOARD
(MOUNT WITH ⅝″ × #6
PAN-HEAD SHEET METAL SCREWS)
(9 REQ'D: 1-BACK/4-EACH SIDE)

12-2. Exploded drawing showing the tail assembly and baseboard.

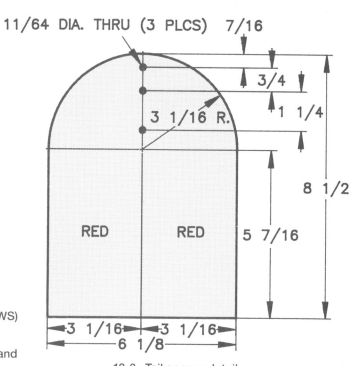

11/64 DIA. THRU (3 PLCS)   7/16

3/4

1 1/4

3 1/16 R.

8 1/2

RED   RED   5 7/16

3 1/16   3 1/16

6 1/8

12-3. Tail spacer detail.

only on the left side of the center wing. Cut out and sand both wings.

Set the drill press table to 15 degrees. Drill a ½″ hole on **one side only** of each of the three wing pieces (12-14). This hole will be used as an alignment hole. Stack the wings and tap a short length (approximately 2″) of ½″ dowel into the holes to pin the wings together. Line the wings up so the leading edges are all parallel, and clamp the wings. Set the drill press table to 15 degrees in the opposite direction, and drill the ½″ hole through the other end of the three wings.

Table 12-1—List of Materials
(Dimensions are for a #1 or T1 rural mailbox)

Quantity	Part	Size of Material
1	Baseboard	*¾ × 6⅛ × 17½
1	Top wing	½ × 5⅜ × 30½
1	Center wing	½ × 4⅜ × 26¾
1	Bottom wing	½ × 4⅜ × 23¼
1	Landing-gear wing	½ × 2¾ × 4¾
2	Landing gear	½ × 2⅝ × 3¼
1	Tail spacer	½ × 6⅛ × 8½
1	Elevator	½ × 6½ × 12
1	Rudder	½ × 5⅝ × 7⅝
1	Cow pilot	½ × 11¾ × 18
1	Propeller	½ × 1⅛ × 9
2	Cleat	¾ × 1⅜ × 4
2	Wood dowel	½ dia. × 18
2	Machine gun barrel	3⁄16 dia. × 1
2	Machine gun	½ dia. × 2⅜
2	Wood wheel	2½ dia. ¾ thick
2	Axle peg	11⁄32 dia. × 1⅝
5	Sheet metal screw	2 × #8
9	Sheet metal screw	⅝ × #6
6	Flat-head wood screw	1 × #8
4	Flat-head wood screw	1¼ × #8
3	Sheet metal screw	½ × #8
1	Mailbox	Size #1 or T1

Exterior enamel paint recommendations: white, brown, grey, pink, red, black.

*Size of baseboard may vary, depending on the brand of mailbox.

Temporarily fasten the bottom wing to the bottom of the mailbox with 1¼″ × #8 flat-head wood screws. The leading edge of the bottom wing is located 2⅞″ back from the front of the mailbox. Cut the ends of the ½″ diameter × 18″ long dowels at a 15-degree angle. See 12–19.

Remove the bolts from the metal catch on top of the mailbox. Assemble the center wing to the bottom wing with the dowels. The center wing should sit on top of the mailbox over the back of the catch. Secure the center wing with ½″ sheet metal screws from inside the mailbox, through the catch holes, through the catch, and into the wings. *Note:* The latches on some mailboxes are riveted. On these, drill out the rivets.

Propeller and Machine Guns

Propeller. Lay out the propeller (12-16) on ½″ plywood and cut out. Drill the ⅛″ pilot hole on the back side of the propeller, approximately 7⁄16″ deep. Position the propeller as shown in 12-19. Drill an 11⁄64″ clearance hole in the door and install the propeller with a ½″ × #8 sheet metal screw (12-15). A flat washer placed under the screw will prevent the tip of the screw from breaking through.

Machine Guns. Build and install the machine guns (12-17–12-18) as follows: Drill a hole 3⁄16″ × ½″ deep into one end of each of the ½″ diameter × 2⅜″ long machine-gun dowels. Glue a 3⁄16″ diameter × 1″ machine-gun barrel in the hole in the end of each machine gun. Glue these completed machine gun assemblies to the top of the wing, approximately 2″ from the center. See 12-15.

Glue the two ½″ diameter dowels to connect the wings in place. Pin the wings and dowels together by drilling a small hole and tapping a 3d finishing nail into the dowels from the front edge of each wing.

Finishing

Sanding. Remove all wood pieces and finish-sand. Fill any voids with wood putty.

Painting. See Chapter 1 for general tips on priming and painting. Color suggestions for this project are given in 12-19 and on drawings for the individual parts. Color recommendations for the cow pilot are in 12-6. The back of the pilot (not shown) is painted white, with a few black "Holstein" spots. Paint a red strip for the scarf and a brown area for the "leather" flying helmet.

Color recommendations for painting the mailbox are in 12-19. It is best to begin with a white metal mailbox.

After all parts are dry, reassemble. Touch up the wood screw heads with the appropriate color of paint.

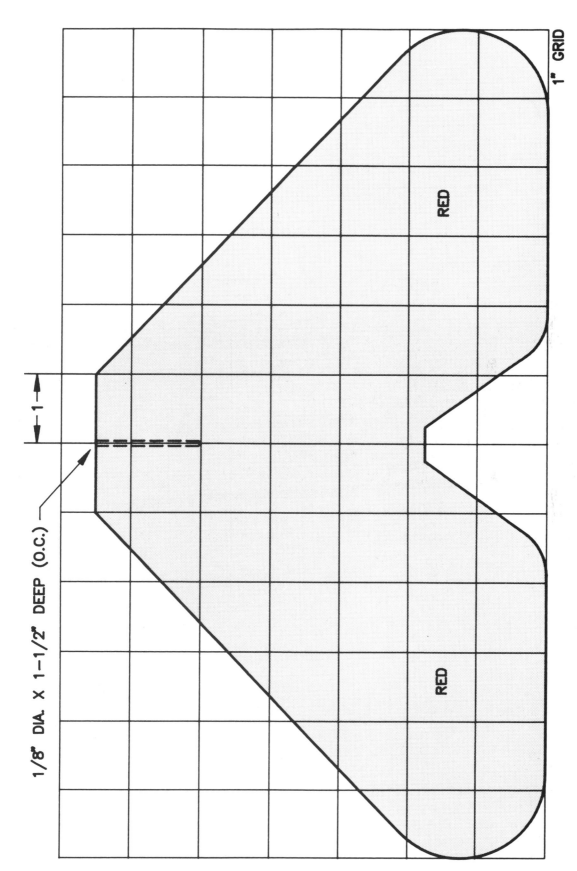

1/8" DIA. X 1-1/2" DEEP (O.C.)

RED

RED

1" GRID

12-4. Elevator detail.

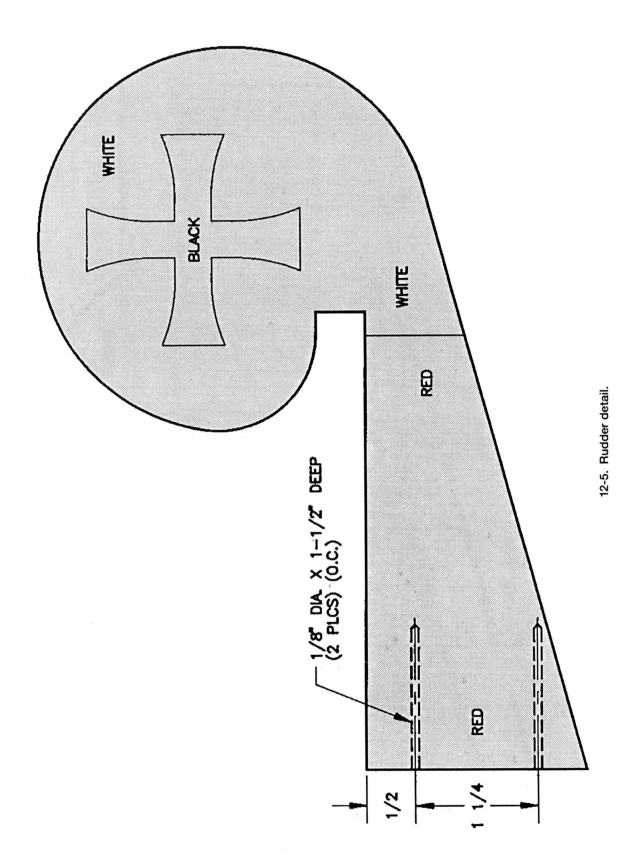

WHITE

BLACK

WHITE

RED

1/8" DIA. X 1-1/2" DEEP (2 PLCS) (O.C.)

RED

1/2

1 1/4

12-5. Rudder detail.

112

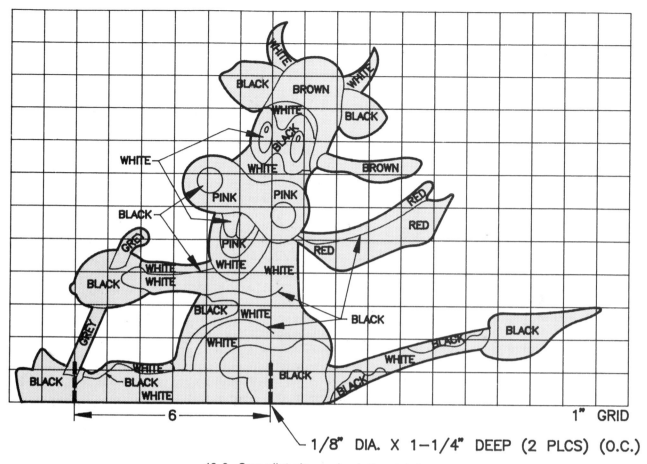

12-6. Cow pilot plan and painting details.

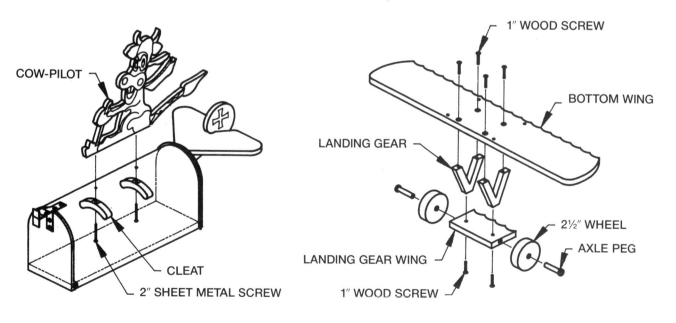

12-7. Exploded assembly drawing showing the installation of the cow pilot with two interior cleats.

12-8. Exploded assembly drawing showing the installation of the bottom wing, landing gear, and landing wing.

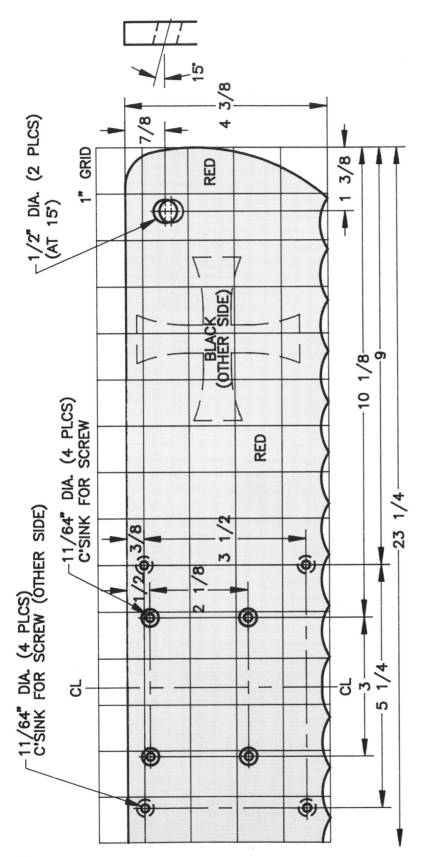

12-9. Bottom wing, detail.

114

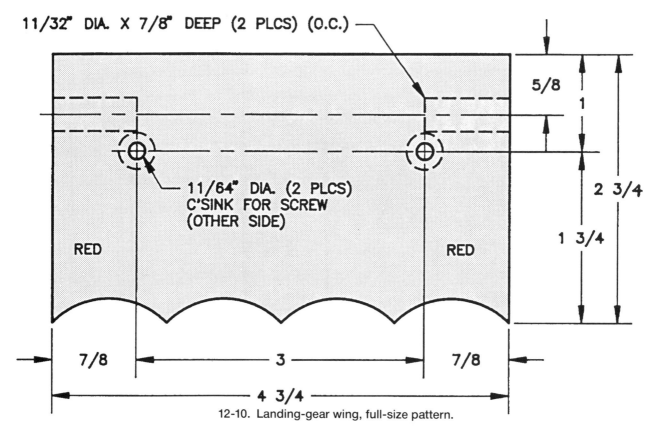

11/32" DIA. X 7/8" DEEP (2 PLCS) (O.C.)

11/64" DIA. (2 PLCS)
C'SINK FOR SCREW
(OTHER SIDE)

RED

RED

5/8

1

2 3/4

1 3/4

7/8

3

7/8

4 3/4

12-10. Landing-gear wing, full-size pattern.

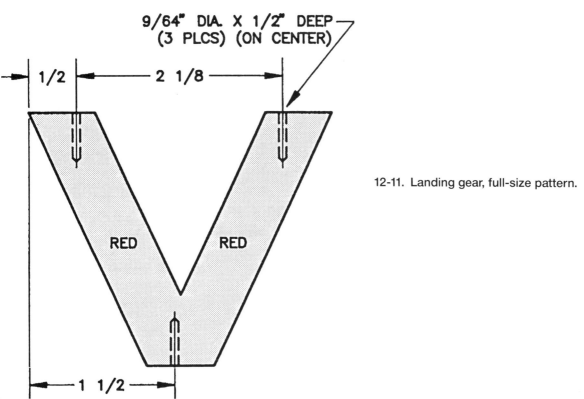

9/64" DIA. X 1/2" DEEP
(3 PLCS) (ON CENTER)

1/2

2 1/8

RED

RED

12-11. Landing gear, full-size pattern.

1 1/2

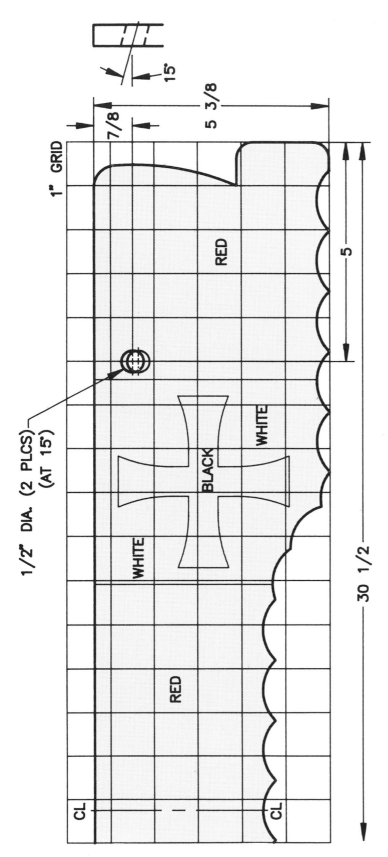

1/2" DIA. (2 PLCS)
(AT 15°)

1" GRID

7/8

5 3/8

RED

WHITE

BLACK

WHITE

RED

5

CL

CL

30 1/2

15°

12-12. Top wing detail.

116

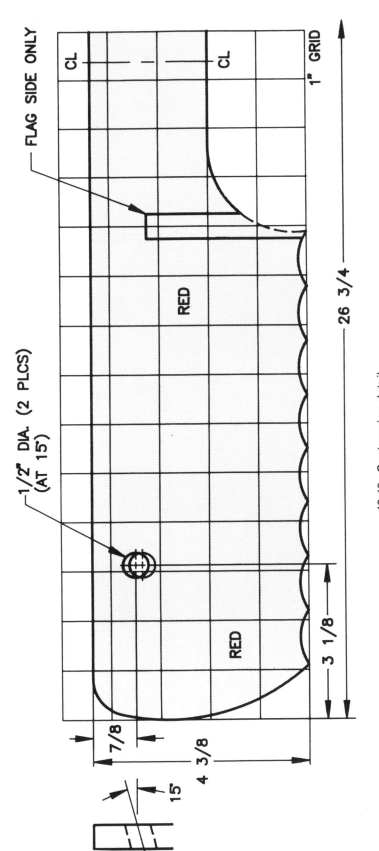

FLAG SIDE ONLY

CL

CL

1" GRID

1/2" DIA. (2 PLCS)
(AT 15°)

RED

RED

26 3/4

3 1/8

7/8

4 3/8

15°

12-13. Center wing detail.

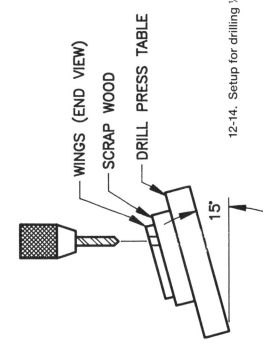

WINGS (END VIEW)

SCRAP WOOD

DRILL PRESS TABLE

15°

12-14. Setup for drilling ½" diameter holes through the wings at 15 degrees.

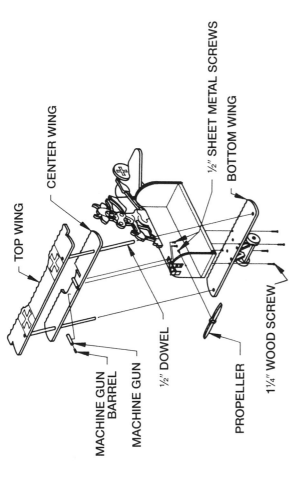

TOP WING

CENTER WING

MACHINE GUN BARREL

MACHINE GUN

½" DOWEL

PROPELLER

1¼" WOOD SCREW

½" SHEET METAL SCREWS

BOTTOM WING

12-15. Exploded drawing showing the assembly of the wings, guns, and propeller.

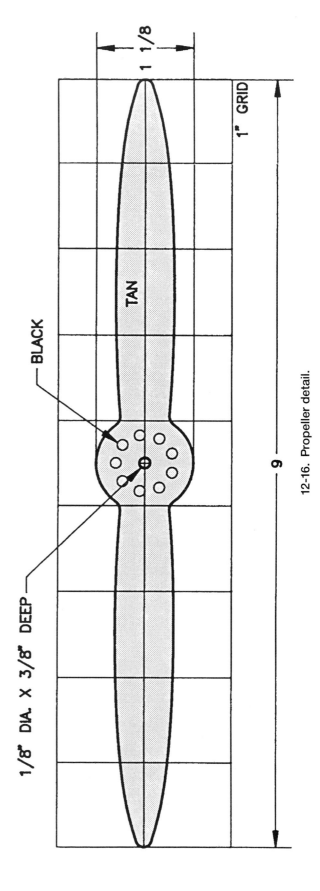

1 1/8

1" GRID

BLACK

TAN

9

1/8" DIA. X 3/8" DEEP

12-16. Propeller detail.

3/16" DIA.

1

12-18. Machine gun barrel detail.

3/16" DIA. X 1/2" DEEP

BLACK

2 3/8

12-17. Machine gun detail.

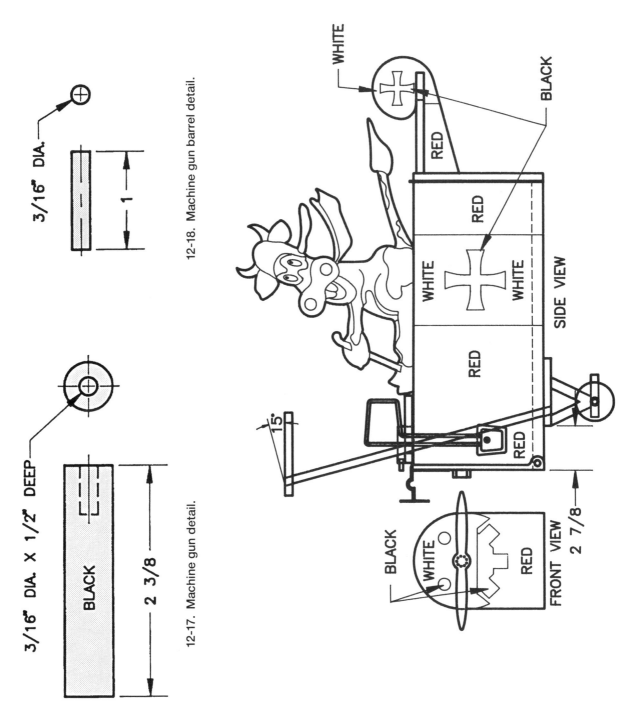

WHITE

RED

BLACK

RED

WHITE

WHITE

RED

SIDE VIEW

15°

RED

BLACK

WHITE

RED

FRONT VIEW

2 7/8

12-19. This illustration gives painting suggestions and shows the location of some parts.

13

Western Saddle

This saddle mailbox is for people who like to ride horses. The shape of the typical rural mailbox lends itself perfectly to this simple design. Optional decorative conchos, available from leather suppliers and saddle shops, provide the perfect visual touch for this western-saddle mailbox. See 13-2, the exploded assembly drawing.

Use a small mailbox. It is helpful to use a pre-painted brown mailbox. Table 13-1 lists all materials required.

Baseboard and Other Parts

Cut a baseboard to fit the recess under your mailbox, and set it aside until later.

The saddle back, saddle front, and horn spacer are all cut from 1½″ thick stock (13-2–13-6). A length of 2 × 6 construction fir is ideal material for making these parts. Lay out the patterns and saw to size with a scroll saw or band saw. *Note:* The saddle horn (13-6) is cut from ¾″ thick stock.

Drill the holes in all pieces, as shown on the patterns. Finish-sand. Drill two ¹¹⁄₆₄″ holes into the top of the mailbox: one hole 3½″ from the front and the other hole 2½″ from the back of the mailbox. The saddle back is fastened over the back hole with a 1″ × #8 screw (13-6).

Before assembling the horn, horn spacer, and saddle front, refer to the side view shown in 13-7. Stack the pieces in position on top of the mailbox. Glue the saddle horn and saddle spacer to the saddle front with exterior glue. Install the entire assembly with a 1″ × #8 sheet metal screw.

Saddle Sides, Stirrups, and Spacers

Enlarge the grid squares to make full-size pat-terns. Cut out right and left pairs for the saddle sides and stirrups (13-8–13-9). Be sure the best side of each part faces outward. Cut two ½″ × 2″ × 12″ spacers (13-10). The spacers hold the saddle sides away from the surface of the mailbox so the flag can operate.

Drill the four holes in each saddle spacer. Drill only the two ⁹⁄₆₄″ holes in each of the saddle sides.

Before attaching the saddle sides and saddle spacer to the mailbox, position a saddle spacer on the back of one of the saddle sides. (Line up the ⁹⁄₆₄″ holes.) To locate the ⅛″ pilot holes to be drilled in the saddle sides, mark through the ¹¹⁄₆₄″ holes in the spacer with a scratch awl. *Note:* 13-2 and 13-8 show these holes as drilled through. If they are drilled through, they will need to be filled after assembly. Instead, you may wish to drill the pilot holes only ⁷⁄₁₆″ deep (from the back of the saddle side). This will eliminate a visible hole on the face of the saddle side.

Place a saddle spacer on one side of the mailbox. Be sure the ¹¹⁄₆₄″ holes are on top. Locate the position of the spacer on the mailbox. It should be 2″ back from the front and even with the bottom of the mailbox. See 13-2.

Use the spacer as a drilling template and drill the holes into the sides of the mailbox. See Chapter 1 for tips on clamping and drilling into the side of the mailbox. Drill the four holes in each side of the mailbox the same diameter called for in the saddle-spacer drawing, 13-10.

Before fastening the saddle sides and side spacer to the mailbox, mount the stirrup pieces to the saddle side. Begin by drilling the two screw clearance holes in each of the stirrup pieces. Remember, the stirrup mounts on the **inside** of the saddle side.

Drill pilot holes and attach with 1″ × #6 screws.

Next, position the baseboard under the mailbox. Hold it in position and mark through each of the ⁹⁄₆₄″ holes drilled in the lip of the mailbox. After marking both holes on each side, drill ⁷⁄₆₄″ pilot holes into the baseboard. Use 2¼″ × #6 screws, as shown in 13-2. These screws go through the ⁹⁄₆₄″ holes in the saddle side, through the holes in the spacer, through the mailbox, and finally into the ⁷⁄₆₄″ holes in the baseboard.

Drive 1″ × #8 sheet metal screws from the inside of the mailbox into the upper pilot holes in the saddle spacer and saddle side. Place a washer under the head of each sheet metal screw, to prevent the screw tip from breaking through.

Finishing

Painting. It is easiest to remove all pieces from the mailbox before painting. Choose a tan or light brown paint for the saddle pieces to contrast with the dark brown paint used on the mailbox. Likewise, the stirrup can be painted a darker brown than the saddle sides for contrast. The lower portion of the stirrups can be painted grey or black.

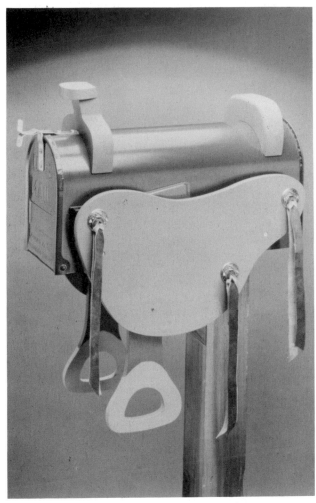

13-1. The Western saddle design evolves easily because of the basic shape of the mailbox.

Table 13-1—List of Materials
(Dimensions are for a #1 or T1 rural mailbox)

Quantity	Part	Size of Material
1	Baseboard	*¾ × 6⅛ × 17½
1	Saddle back	1½ × 3¾ × 6¼
1	Saddle front	1½ × 3½ × 6¼
1	Horn spacer	1¼ × 1½ × 1⅞
1	Saddle horn	¾ × 2⅜ × 2¾
2	Saddle side	½ × 10¼ × 17¾
2	Saddle spacer	½ × 2 × 12
2	Saddle stirrup	½ × 5½ × 10½
6	Concho	1½ dia.
6	Leather strap	⅝ × 24
6	Sheet metal screw	1 × #8
4	Trim-head drywall screw	2¼ × #6
4	Wood screw	1 × #6
12	Rd. hd. wood screw	½ × #4
1	Mailbox	Size #1 or T1

Recommended exterior enamel paint colors: brown, dark brown, grey.

*Size of baseboard may vary, depending on the brand of mailbox.

Conchos. Saddle adornments such as conchos can be added for a final touch. The conchos shown in 13-1 and 13-11 are 1½″ in diameter. The suede strips are ⅝″ wide and hang down about 12 inches.

Conchos and suede strips are available at leather and saddle shops. When visiting such a shop, you may wish to bring this book along, to give them an idea of what you are looking for. The shop we visited let us select the color suede we liked best, then they cut the strips for us and attached them to the metal conchos, all for around $2.00 each.

To mount the finished concho adornments, drill a ⁷⁄₆₄″ hole in both sides of each metal concho and attach them to the saddle sides with ½″ × #4 round-head wood screws at the general locations shown in 13-1.

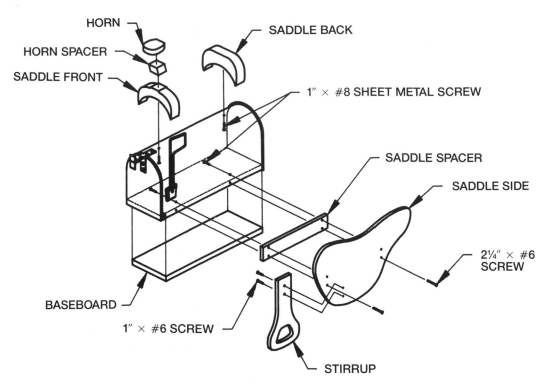

HORN

HORN SPACER

SADDLE FRONT

SADDLE BACK

1″ × #8 SHEET METAL SCREW

SADDLE SPACER

SADDLE SIDE

2¼″ × #6 SCREW

BASEBOARD

1″ × #6 SCREW

STIRRUP

13-2. Exploded assembly drawing shows the position of the various parts.

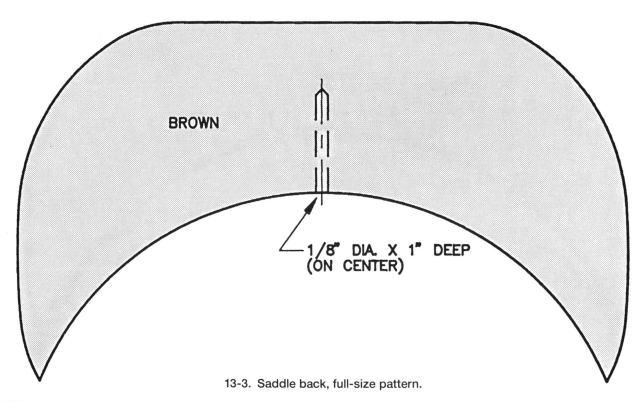

BROWN

1/8″ DIA. X 1″ DEEP
(ON CENTER)

13-3. Saddle back, full-size pattern.

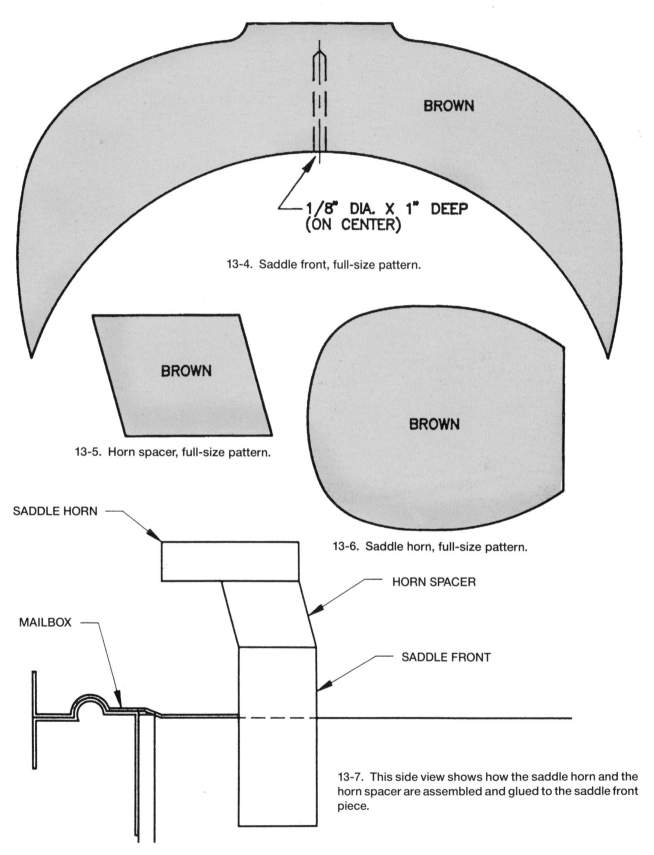

BROWN

1/8" DIA. X 1" DEEP
(ON CENTER)

13-4. Saddle front, full-size pattern.

BROWN

13-5. Horn spacer, full-size pattern.

BROWN

13-6. Saddle horn, full-size pattern.

SADDLE HORN

HORN SPACER

MAILBOX

SADDLE FRONT

13-7. This side view shows how the saddle horn and the horn spacer are assembled and glued to the saddle front piece.

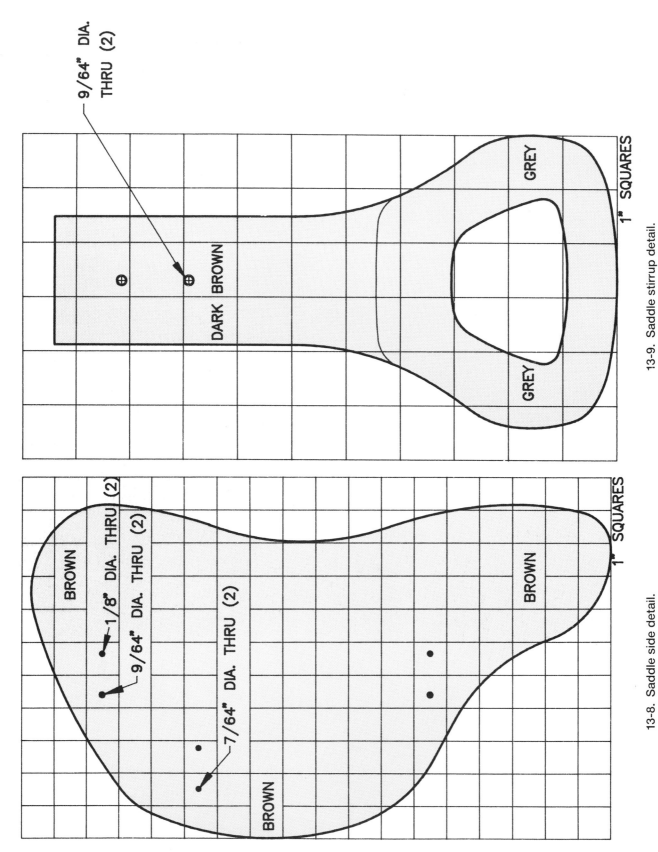

9/64" DIA. THRU (2)

DARK BROWN

GREY

GREY

1" SQUARES

13-9. Saddle stirrup detail.

BROWN

1/8" DIA. THRU (2)

9/64" DIA. THRU (2)

7/64" DIA. THRU (2)

BROWN

BROWN

1" SQUARES

13-8. Saddle side detail.

124

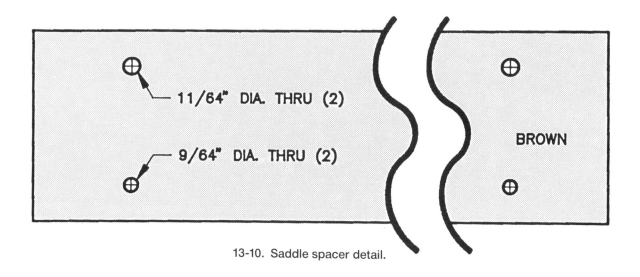

11/64" DIA. THRU (2)

9/64" DIA. THRU (2)

BROWN

13-10. Saddle spacer detail.

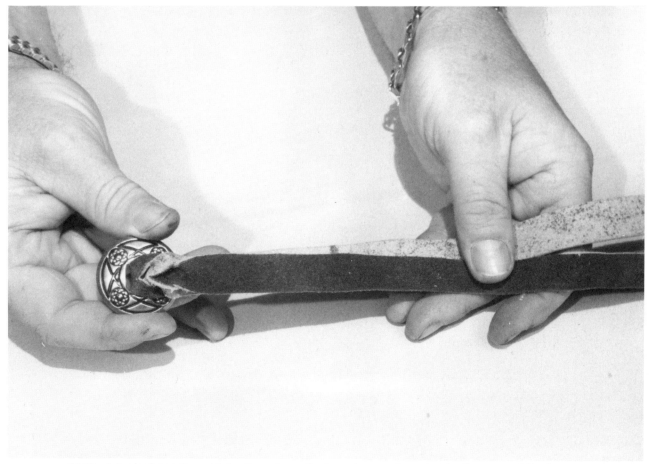

13-11. A typical concho with leather straps that can be purchased at leather or saddle shops.

14
Horse Trailer

This mailbox is perfect for people who own horses or who would like to own horses. Race horses, riding horses, or rodeo horses, they are all transported by horse trailer.

There are relatively few pieces required, which makes this project particularly easy. See the exploded assembly drawing, 14-2. The windows are done with automotive striping tape. The wheels are doll-stroller wheels. The horse "rear ends" are painted on. People especially like the plywood tails, which give the project just the right finishing touch. Start with a prepainted mailbox in the color of your choice. Table 14-1 lists all materials required.

Baseboard

Cut the baseboard to fit the recess under your mailbox. Attach the baseboard temporarily with several small screws driven through the lower lip.

Wheels

Selecting the Wheels. We chose 4¼″ wheels, the kind used on doll strollers, because they are the right size, look good, and are inexpensive. You can order them by mail, or you might be able to salvage wheels from an old stroller. You could also make your own wheels from wood. See Chapter 8. Use the wheel shown on page 66.

Fenders and Axle Block

Fenders. Once you have the wheels, proceed with construction of the fenders (14-3). The pattern could be enlarged or reduced for wheels slightly larger or smaller than the ones we used. Cut one fender piece for each side of the mailbox from ¾″ plywood or solid wood stock.

Axle Blocks. The axle blocks (14-4) are also cut from ¾″ thick material. Remember to drill the axle holes in these blocks the same size (or ¹⁄₆₄″ larger) as the axle holes in the wheels. Drill the ¹¹⁄₆₄″ clearance holes, which will be used to fasten these pieces to the baseboard, as shown.

Assemble Fenders and Axle Block. To determine where the fenders and axle block will be attached, bolt the wheels to one of the axle blocks, then hold the axle block and fender on the flag side of the mailbox. The front of the fender should be about 3″ back from the front of the mailbox. The ends of the fenders extend below the mailbox about 1″. Note that on mailboxes with large flags, the flag may hit the top of the fender. By mounting the fender as low as possible you will provide maximum clearance for the flag. Don't mount the fender so low that it touches the tops of the wheels.

When you are satisfied with the position, mark the location of both the fender and the axle block. Remove the wheels and attach the axle block to the baseboard with 2½″ × #8 screws (14-2). Recheck the location of the fenders in relation to the wheels; drill ¹¹⁄₆₄″ clearance holes through the metal mailbox; and drill ⅛″ pilot holes in the fenders. The fenders are attached with ½″ × #8 sheet metal screws installed from inside the mailbox.

Horse Tails and Trailer Hitch

Horse Tails. The horse tails (14-5) are mounted on the door of the mailbox so they are easily seen. Cut both tails from ½″ plywood. Fasten the tails to the

14-1. This horse trailer mailbox has much significance for ranchers and horse lovers.

mailbox door with ½″ × #8 sheet metal screws. The location for the ¹¹⁄₆₄″ clearance holes in the door is given in 14-6.

Trailer Hitch. Cut the trailer hitch (14-7) from ½″ plywood. The trailer hitch is attached to the bottom of the baseboard and it extends outward from the back end of the mailbox. A ⁷⁄₃₂″ diameter hole for a hitch pin is drilled through the hitch for a small wooden toy axle peg that is driven in later for appearance. Drill two ⁹⁄₆₄″ clearance holes through the hitch for mounting it to the baseboard. Fasten the hitch piece so 2″ is under the baseboard, leaving just the triangular area exposed. Tap the ⁷⁄₃₂″ toy axle peg approximately half way into the hitch hole.

Finishing

Disassemble all wood pieces and prepare them for priming. The colors used for the areas above what would be the tailgate and the horse rear views are painted directly on the door of the metal mailbox so they stand out visually (14-6). Always select color combinations that contrast, so they will stand out.

Table 14-1—List of Materials
(Dimensions are for a #1 or T1 rural mailbox)

Quantity	Part	Size of Material
1	Baseboard	*¾ × 6⅛ × 17½
2	Fender	¾ × 3½ × 12½
2	Axle block	¾ × 2 × 8
1	Trailer hitch	½ × 6 × 6¼
2	Horse tail	½ × 1⅝ × 5⅛
1	Toy axle peg	⁷⁄₃₂ dia.
Misc.	Auto striping tape	³⁄₁₆ wide
4	Wheel	4¼ dia.
4	Bolt	¼ dia. × 2¼ long
4	Nut	To fit bolts
4	Wood screw	2½ × #8
8	Sheet metal screw	½ × #8
2	Wood screw	1 × #6
1	Mailbox	Size #1 or T1

Exterior enamel paint recommendations: brown, grey, black, white.

*Size of baseboard may vary, depending on the brand of mailbox.

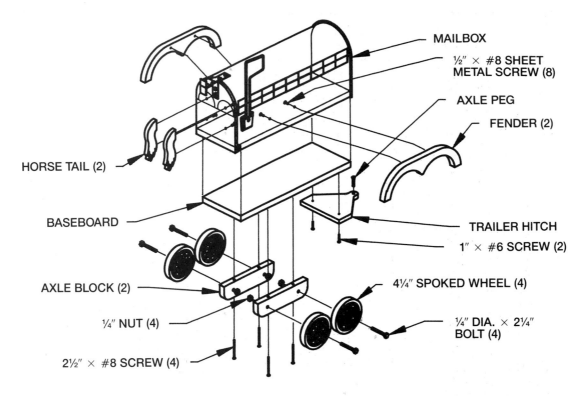

MAILBOX

½″ × #8 SHEET
METAL SCREW (8)

AXLE PEG

FENDER (2)

HORSE TAIL (2)

BASEBOARD

TRAILER HITCH

1″ × #6 SCREW (2)

AXLE BLOCK (2)

4¼″ SPOKED WHEEL (4)

¼″ NUT (4)

¼″ DIA. × 2¼″
BOLT (4)

2½″ × #8 SCREW (4)

14-2. This exploded assembly drawing shows all the parts for the horse trailer mailbox.

If using a standard silver or galvanized mailbox, almost any dark colors will contrast well. See Chapter 1 for tips on painting wood and metal surfaces.

On the door, paint the area above the horses black. Paint the horses' rears and tails at this time.

Paint the fenders and hitch piece before reassembly.

Window details are created using automotive striping tape. See 14-8 for the size and layout for the windows. Mark the window layout directly onto the mailbox using a pencil and square. Use ³⁄₁₆″ wide colored striping tape, applying the short vertical strips 2″ apart first. Complete the window detail by applying the horizontal stripes, covering the ends of the vertical pieces.

Final Assembly

Reassemble all pieces. Bolt the wheels to the axle block. The use of axles is not recommended in this project because they may get in the way when mounting the project to a post.

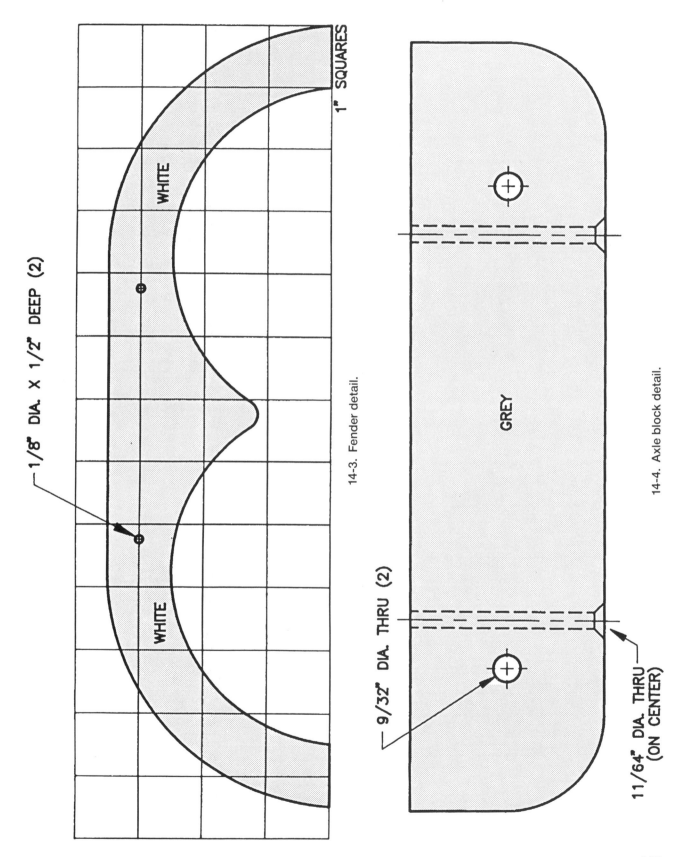

1/8" DIA. X 1/2" DEEP (2)

WHITE

WHITE

1" SQUARES

14-3. Fender detail.

9/32" DIA. THRU (2)

GREY

11/64" DIA. THRU
(ON CENTER)

14-4. Axle block detail.

129

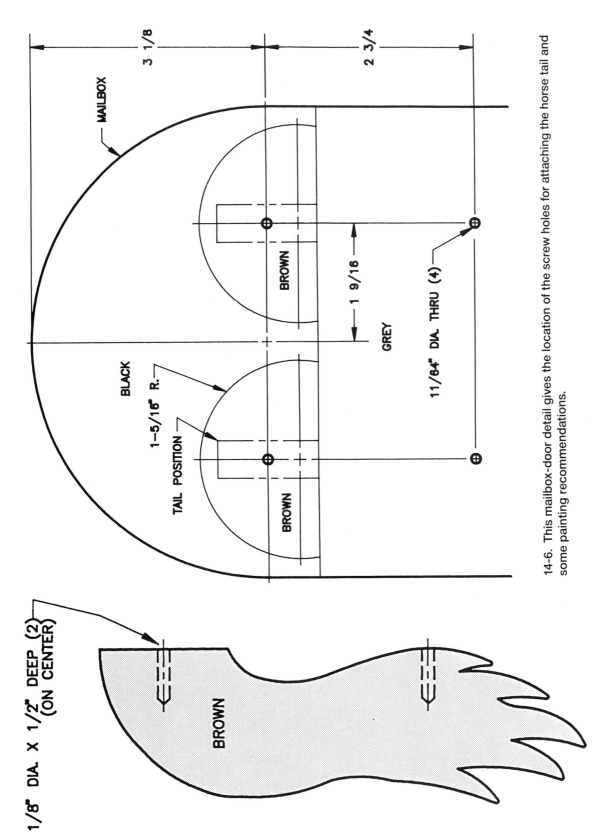

3 1/8

2 3/4

MAILBOX

BROWN

GREY

1 9/16

11/64" DIA. THRU (4)

BLACK

1-5/16" R.

TAIL POSITION

BROWN

14-6. This mailbox-door detail gives the location of the screw holes for attaching the horse tail and some painting recommendations.

1/8" DIA. X 1/2" DEEP (2) (ON CENTER)

BROWN

14-5. Horse tail, full-size pattern.

130

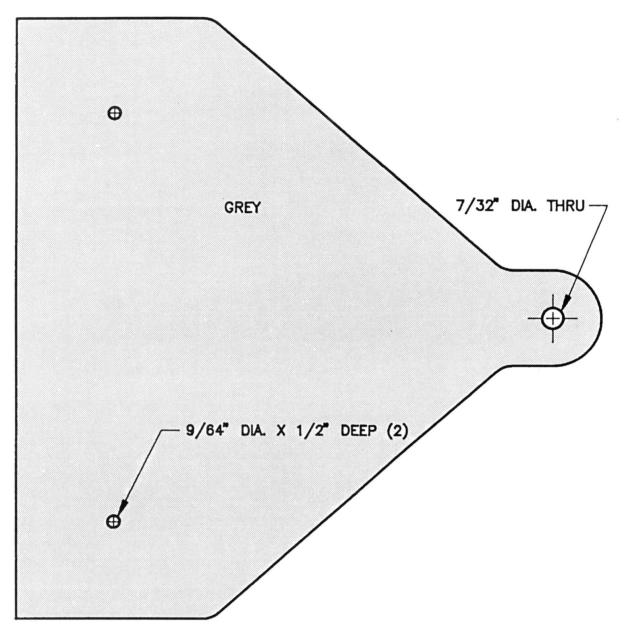

GREY

7/32" DIA. THRU

9/64" DIA. X 1/2" DEEP (2)

14-7. Trailer hitch, full-size pattern.

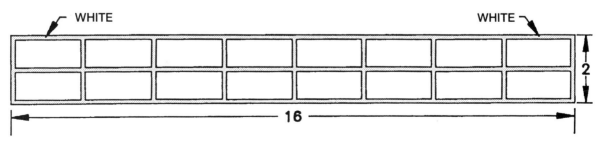

WHITE   WHITE

2

16

14-8. Window detail layout for automotive striping tape application.

15
Church

The country church exemplifies America's freedom of worship. This project could represent churches of almost any denomination.

The project can be built using any of the three standard-size rural mailboxes. The dimensions given in the list of materials (Table 15-1) are for building a church that will fit over a standard small-size mailbox. See drawings in 15-5 and 15-6. With a medium or large mailbox, the church will obviously be larger. Refer to the drawings to determine the actual cutting sizes needed for building larger church mailboxes.

If you plan to paint your mailbox white, save time by purchasing a white prepainted one. Optional decorative plastic windows and cedar shakes add classic finishing touches.

Table 15-1 lists all materials required.

Front, Back, Sides, and Base

Baseboard. Cut the baseboard to fit the recess under the mailbox. Attach the baseboard temporarily with two or more small screws in each side. Remove the flag assembly from the mailbox and set it aside.

Church Front/Back. Refer to the drawings for the front/back parts that correspond to your mailbox size. See 15-5–15-6. Lay out and transfer the pattern for the small or medium church front and back pieces onto ½″ stock (15-4). *Note:* If the church will accommodate the large mailbox, use 15-6. The front and back pieces are identical for each size project, except that an opening to receive the metal mailbox is cut in the front piece only. Cut and finish-sand the front and back pieces.

Church Base and Sides. The dimensions for the church base (15-7) and sides (15-8) are given in the drawings for each particular size of project. Lay out the church base and two sides, and cut from ½″ stock to the size that corresponds to the mailbox size you are using.

Fasten the sides and church back to the church base with finishing nails and exterior glue. See 15-2. Insert the mailbox inside the church cavity. The front piece will fit over the mailbox and automatically center it. *Important:* The mailbox should be positioned so that the front extends approximately 1″ beyond the front of the church base. Open the mailbox door all the way to check that it opens freely.

Attach the church base to the baseboard with two 1″ × #8 wood screws (installed from the bottom). Then glue and nail the church front to the sides and church base.

Roof, Chimney, and Steeple

Roof. Lay out and cut the church roof from ½″ stock (15-10). Only the right side of the roof requires an opening for the chimney. Finish-sand the roof pieces and attach them with finishing nails and exterior glue. See 15-3.

Chimney. Lay out and cut the chimney from a 2 × 4″ (15-9). Finish-sand the chimney and glue in place.

Steeple. All the steeple parts are made from ¼″ thick material. Lay out and cut the front, back, two sides (15-11–15-12), and the bell mount.

A 1″ brass church bell can be hung in the steeple for the crowning touch. This bell can be attached with a small screw eye screwed into the bell mount.

Finish-sand all wood steeple pieces, and assemble the steeple front, back, sides, and bell mount with small wire brads and glue. See 15-3. Toe-nail and glue the steeple assembly to the church roof, approximately 4″ from the front.

Lay out and cut the steeple roofs and cross from ¼″ stock. Finish-sand these pieces, and assemble with wire brads and exterior glue. Glue the cross in the notch in the steeple roof. See 15-4.

Finishing

Painting. The church front, back, and sides are painted white. Use a contrasting color for the roof, roof edges, and roof undersides on both the church and the steeple. It is best to avoid painting precut plastic decorative windows, because paint may not adhere well. The windows we used were made from

Table 15-1—List of Materials

(Dimensions given below are for building the small church using a small mailbox. For larger mailboxes, refer to the individual drawings for dimensions of the pieces.)

Quantity	Part	Size of Material
1	Baseboard	*¾ × 6⅛ × 17½
2	Church front/back	½ × 10¼ × 14⅝
1	Church base	½ × 10¼ × 18⅜
2	Church side	½ × 8½ × 17⅜
2	Church roof	½ × 12 × 20⅜
1	Chimney	1½ × 3½ × 12
2	Steeple front/back	¼ × 2 × 4¹¹⁄₁₆
2	Steeple side	¼ × 1½ × 3½
1	Bell mount	¼ × 1½ × 1½
2	Steeple roof	¼ × 2½ × 3
1	Cross	¼ × 1½ × 3
9	Sheet metal screw	⅝ × #6
1	Screw eye	¼ dia. × ½
1	Round bell	1
10	Plastic window	⅛ × 1½ × 3½
40	Escutcheon pins	⅜ × #18
2	Wood screw	1 × #8
1	Sheet metal screw	1 × #8
Pkg.	Cedar shakes	1000 pcs.
1	Mailbox	Size #1 or T1

Exterior enamel paint color recommendations: black, white, yellow.

*Size of baseboard may vary, depending on the brand of mailbox.

15-1. This church can be made to fit around a #1-size standard mailbox, or around either of two other larger metal mailboxes.

polypropylene plastic, which has a slippery surface. A permanent-ink felt pen can be used to darken the window to create more contrast.

Before nailing windows in place, you may wish to paint the rectangular area behind each window bright yellow. For the small-mailbox church, place two windows in the front, two in the back, and three on each side. With the medium or large mailbox, no room will remain for front windows. In this case, place two windows in the back and four windows on each side.

Final Assembly

To attach cedar shakes to the church roof (15-4), begin by drawing a horizontal line approximately 1″ from the bottom edge of the roof. Continue draw-

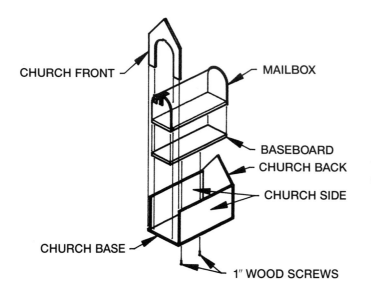

CHURCH FRONT

MAILBOX

BASEBOARD

CHURCH BACK

CHURCH SIDE

CHURCH BASE

1" WOOD SCREWS

15-2. Exploded assembly drawing of the basic church structure.

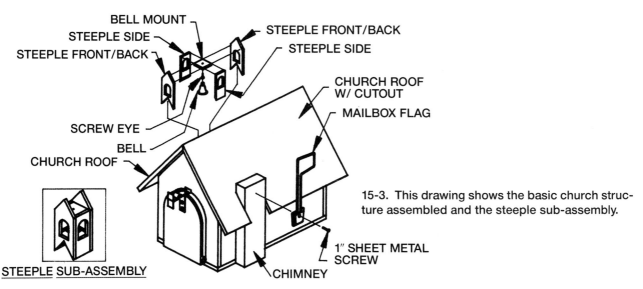

BELL MOUNT

STEEPLE SIDE

STEEPLE FRONT/BACK

STEEPLE FRONT/BACK

STEEPLE SIDE

CHURCH ROOF W/ CUTOUT

MAILBOX FLAG

SCREW EYE

BELL

CHURCH ROOF

STEEPLE SUB-ASSEMBLY

1" SHEET METAL SCREW

CHIMNEY

15-3. This drawing shows the basic church structure assembled and the steeple sub-assembly.

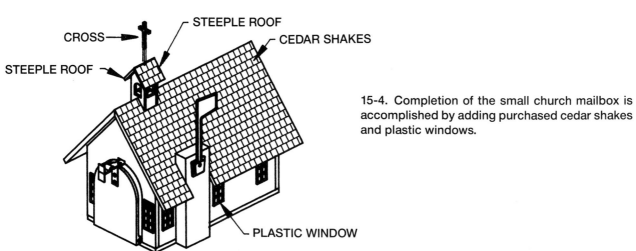

CROSS

STEEPLE ROOF

CEDAR SHAKES

STEEPLE ROOF

PLASTIC WINDOW

15-4. Completion of the small church mailbox is accomplished by adding purchased cedar shakes and plastic windows.

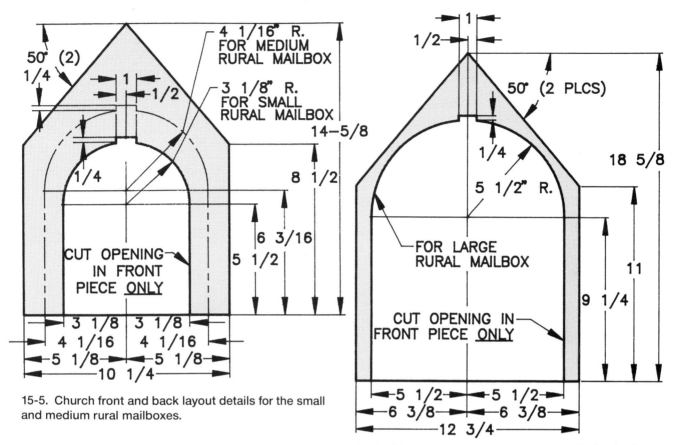

50° (2)
1/4
1
1/2
4 1/16" R.
FOR MEDIUM
RURAL MAILBOX

3 1/8" R.
FOR SMALL
RURAL MAILBOX

14—5/8

1/4

8 1/2

CUT OPENING
IN FRONT
PIECE ONLY

6 3/16

5 1/2

3 1/8   3 1/8
4 1/16   4 1/16
5 1/8   5 1/8
10 1/4

15-5. Church front and back layout details for the small and medium rural mailboxes.

1
1/2
50° (2 PLCS)
1/4
5 1/2" R.
18 5/8
FOR LARGE
RURAL MAILBOX
11
CUT OPENING IN
FRONT PIECE ONLY
9 1/4

5 1/2   5 1/2
6 3/8   6 3/8
12 3/4

15-6. Church front and back layout details for the large rural mailbox.

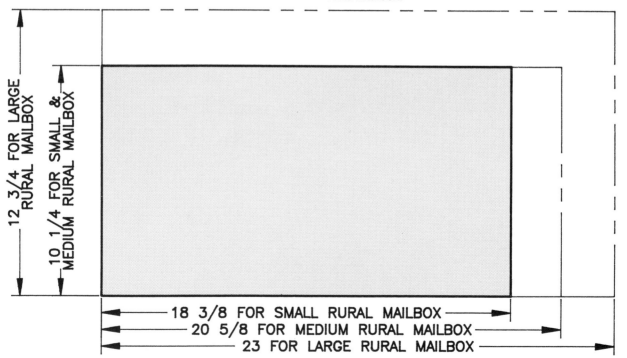

12 3/4 FOR LARGE RURAL MAILBOX

10 1/4 FOR SMALL & MEDIUM RURAL MAILBOX

18 3/8 FOR SMALL RURAL MAILBOX
20 5/8 FOR MEDIUM RURAL MAILBOX
23 FOR LARGE RURAL MAILBOX

15-7. Church base, layout details.

ing horizontal lines in 1″ increments, working towards the peak of the roof. The spaces can be adjusted slightly so the last line comes out 1″ below the peak of the roof. These guidelines help locate the position of the shakes. Place a bead of silicone or construction adhesive across the length of the bottom line using a caulk gun. Press the cedar shakes in place, so that approximately ¼″ of the shake extends over the bottom edge of the roof.

Continue this procedure, always positioning the next row of shakes to overlap the row below it by approximately ¼″. Protect cedar shakes with several coats of moisture-repellent clear penetrating sealer or paint.

Mount the mailbox flag near the top of the chimney. Mark and drill holes where needed in the flag mount and attach the flag assembly with 1″ × #8 sheet metal screw(s). See 15-3.

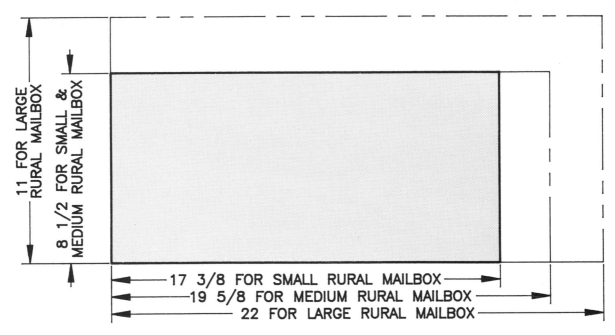

11 FOR LARGE RURAL MAILBOX

8 1/2 FOR SMALL & MEDIUM RURAL MAILBOX

17 3/8 FOR SMALL RURAL MAILBOX
19 5/8 FOR MEDIUM RURAL MAILBOX
22 FOR LARGE RURAL MAILBOX

15-8. Church side, layout details.

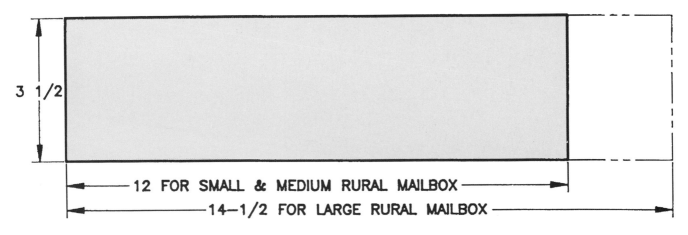

3 1/2

12 FOR SMALL & MEDIUM RURAL MAILBOX
14—1/2 FOR LARGE RURAL MAILBOX

15-9. Chimney.

136

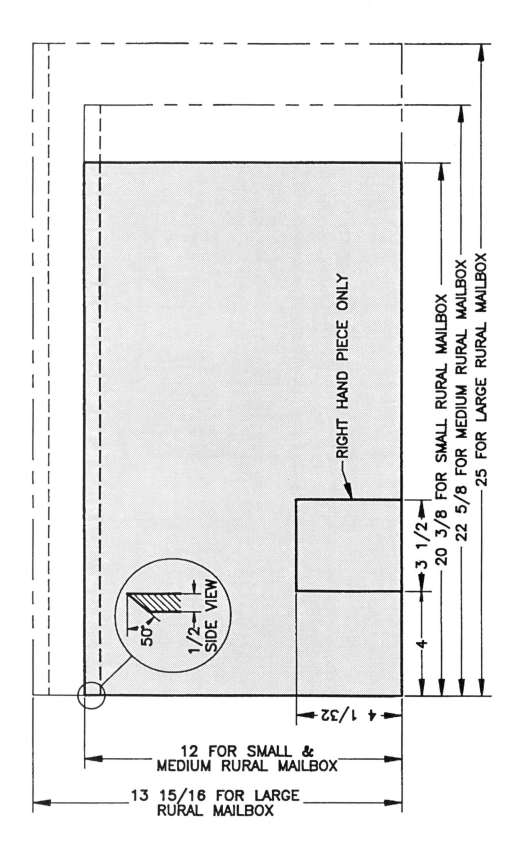

RIGHT HAND PIECE ONLY

SIDE VIEW

50°

1/2

4 1/32

3 1/2

4

20 3/8 FOR SMALL RURAL MAILBOX

22 5/8 FOR MEDIUM RURAL MAILBOX

25 FOR LARGE RURAL MAILBOX

12 FOR SMALL &
MEDIUM RURAL MAILBOX

13 15/16 FOR LARGE
RURAL MAILBOX

15-10. Church roof, layout details.

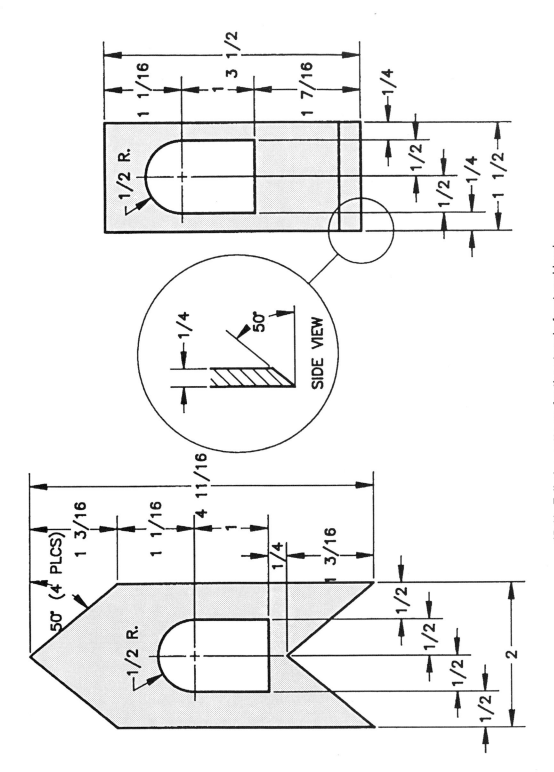

15-11. Full-size patterns for the steeple front and back.

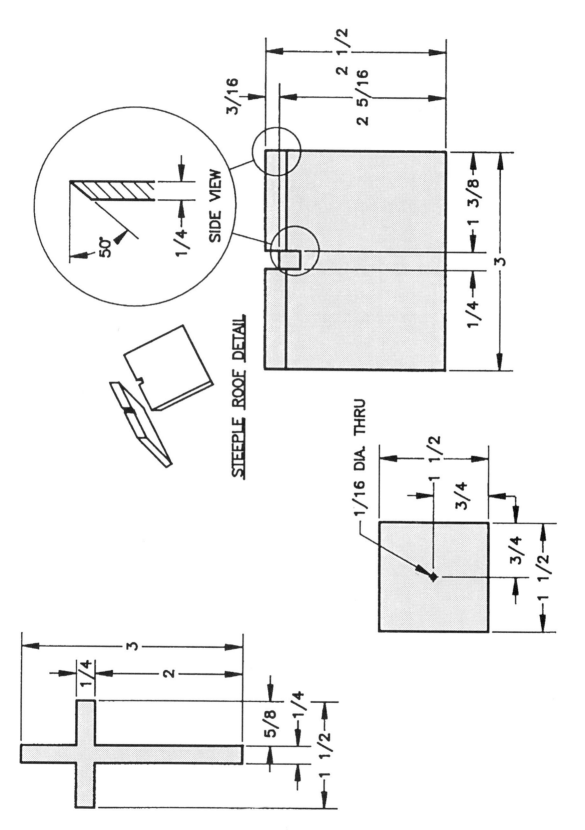

3/16

2 1/2

2 5/16

2

SIDE VIEW

50°

1/4

1 3/8

3

1/4

STEEPLE ROOF DETAIL

1/16 DIA. THRU

1/2

3/4

3/4

1 1/2

1

3

1/4

2

5/8

1/4

1 1/2

1

15-12. Full-size patterns for the steeple roof pieces, the bell mount, and the cross.

139

16
Barn

Distinctive to American tradition, the barn has become a well-known symbol of the family farm. Built to protect animals and to store hay, these historic structures are slowly being replaced by modern steel structures. This project is designed to accommodate a small, medium, or large mailbox. The outside dimensions of the front and back pieces are the same, regardless of which mailbox is used. The front is large enough to accommodate even the largest mailbox. The roof, side pieces, and base are all marked with three different lengths, to correspond to the different sizes of mailboxes. Decorative plastic windows and cedar shakes add a classic finishing touch.

Table 16-1 lists the materials required.

Cutting the Parts

Assembly drawings 16-2–16-3 show the basic structural parts and assembly.

Baseboard. Cut out the baseboard to fit the recess under the mailbox. Attach the baseboard with two or more small screws in each side.

Remove the flag assembly from the mailbox and set it aside.

Front, Back, Sides and Base. Transfer the barn front pattern (16-4) onto ½″ stock and cut out. Cut an opening to match the size of the mailbox. Transfer the barn base (16-5), barn rear (16-6), barn left and right sides (16-7–16-8), and the shed side (16-9) patterns onto ½″ stock and cut out.

Finish-sand and assemble the barn sides, shed side, and barn rear piece to the barn base with finishing nails and exterior glue. See 16-2.

Position and center the metal mailbox inside the barn cavity using the barn front as a guide. The mailbox should extend approximately 1″ beyond the front of the barn base. Open the mailbox door all the way and check that it opens freely. Attach the mailbox baseboard to the barn base with two 1″ wood screws (installed from the bottom).

Attach the barn front to the barn sides and base with finishing nails and glue.

Roof. Lay out and cut the barn roof (16-10–16-12) and the shed roof (16-13) to size from ½″ stock. Finish-sand and attach the roof pieces with finishing nails and glue. See 16-3.

Cupolas and Flag Mount. Lay out and cut the cupolas (16-14) from 2″ thick solid stock. Lay out and cut the flag mount (16-15) from ¾″ thick stock. Finish-sand and attach the cupolas to the barn roof. Center approximately 4″ in from each end of the roof. Attach the flag mount to the barn right side, as shown in 16-16. The center of the flag mount should be approximately 1½″ from the front and 6″ from the bottom of the side of the barn. The cupolas and flag mount are secured with glue and small nails.

Finishing

Painting. Paint all plywood pieces with two coats of latex primer followed by a finishing coat of exterior-gloss or semi-gloss latex enamel. Paint the project "barn red," except for the roof pieces, which are painted white.

Before nailing the windows in place, paint the rectangular area behind each window black. Attach the windows with small brass nails. *Note:* For the small or medium mailbox, place two windows on the front and two or three windows on each side. With the large mailbox, there will not be room for windows in the front.

16-1. This barn mailbox features an attached shed, which functions as a receptacle for newspaper delivery. The project plans allow for a choice of three mailbox sizes: the standard, the medium, or the large size.

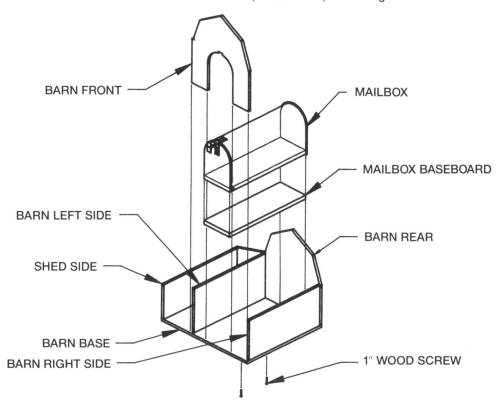

BARN FRONT

MAILBOX

MAILBOX BASEBOARD

BARN LEFT SIDE

SHED SIDE

BARN REAR

BARN BASE

BARN RIGHT SIDE

1″ WOOD SCREW

16-2. Exploded assembly drawing shows the barn substructure cavity, which cradles the metal mailbox liner.

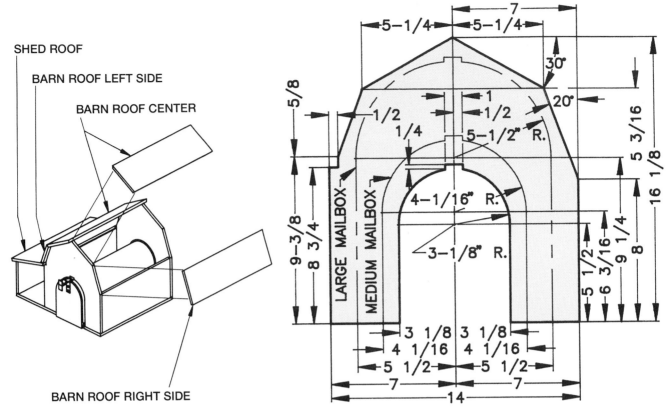

SHED ROOF

BARN ROOF LEFT SIDE

BARN ROOF CENTER

BARN ROOF RIGHT SIDE

16-3. Roof assembly. Roof boards overlap the structure by 1″ on each end.

16-4. Barn front: layout details for three different mailbox sizes.

Table 16-1—List of Materials

(Dimensions given below are for the small barn using a #1 or T1 rural mailbox. For larger mailboxes, refer to the individual drawings for the dimensions of the pieces.)

Quantity	Part	Size of Material	Quantity	Part	Size of Material
1	Baseboard	*¾ × 6⅛ × 17½	1	Barn roof left side	½ × 4¼ × 19⅞
1	Barn front	½ × 14 × 16⅛	1	Shed roof	½ × 8 × 19⅞
1	Barn base	½ × 18⅜ × 21	2	Cupola	2 × 2 × 2
1	Barn rear	½ × 16⅛ × 21	1	Flag mount	¾ × 2⅛ × 2⅛
1	Barn left side	½ × 8¾ × 17⅜	Misc.	Sheet metal screw	1 × #8
1	Barn right side	½ × 8 × 17⅜	8	Plastic window	⅛ × 1½ × 3½
1	Shed side	½ × 6⅞ × 17⅞	3	Wood screw	1 × #8
1	Barn roof right side	½ × 6½ × 19⅞	Pkg.	Cedar shakes	1000 pcs.
2	Barn roof center	½ × 6⅜ × 19⅞	1	Mailbox	Size #1 or T1

Exterior enamel paint recommendations: barn red and white.

*Size of baseboard may vary, depending on the brand of mailbox.

142

Final Assembly

Cedar Shakes. Cedar shakes are applied in the same manner as described for the church project. See 16-16 and refer to Chapter 15, pages 133–134.

Flag. Mark and drill holes where needed and attach the flag assembly to the flag mount with 1″ × #8 sheet metal screw(s).

16-5. Base: layout details for three different mailbox project sizes.

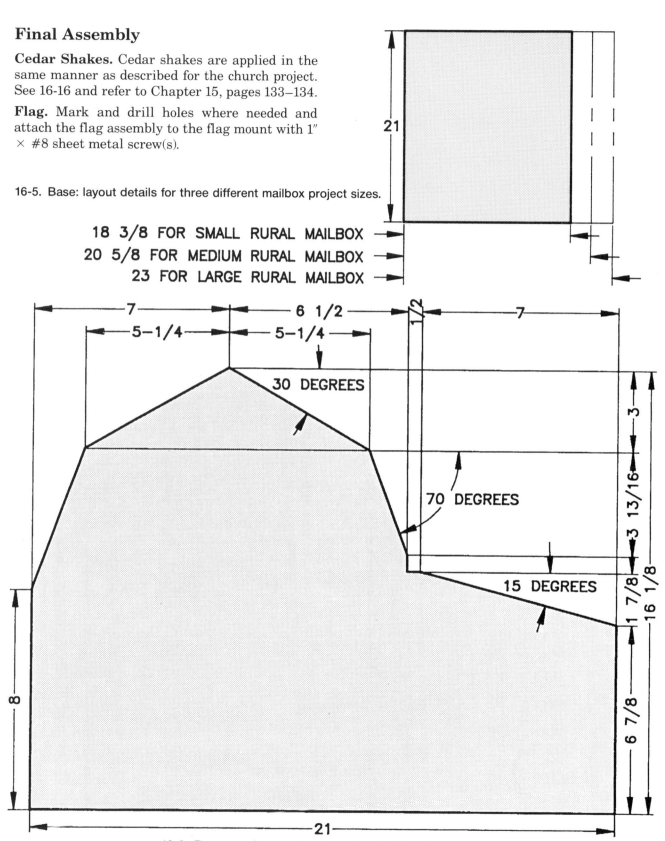

21

18 3/8 FOR SMALL RURAL MAILBOX →
20 5/8 FOR MEDIUM RURAL MAILBOX →
23 FOR LARGE RURAL MAILBOX →

7   6 1/2   1/2   7

5-1/4   5-1/4

30 DEGREES

70 DEGREES

15 DEGREES

3

3 13/16

1 7/8

16 1/8

6 7/8

8

21

16-6. Barn rear: layout details are identical for all three sizes.

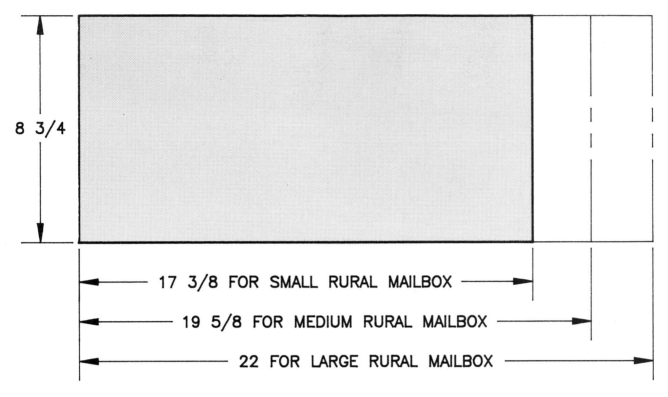

8 3/4

17 3/8 FOR SMALL RURAL MAILBOX

19 5/8 FOR MEDIUM RURAL MAILBOX

22 FOR LARGE RURAL MAILBOX

16-7. Barn left side: layout details for three sizes.

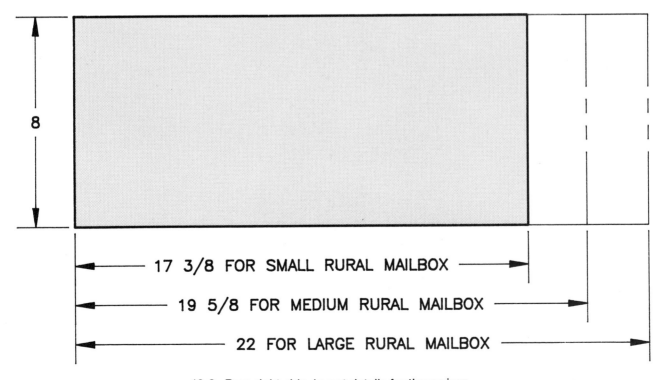

8

17 3/8 FOR SMALL RURAL MAILBOX

19 5/8 FOR MEDIUM RURAL MAILBOX

22 FOR LARGE RURAL MAILBOX

16-8. Barn right side: layout details for three sizes.

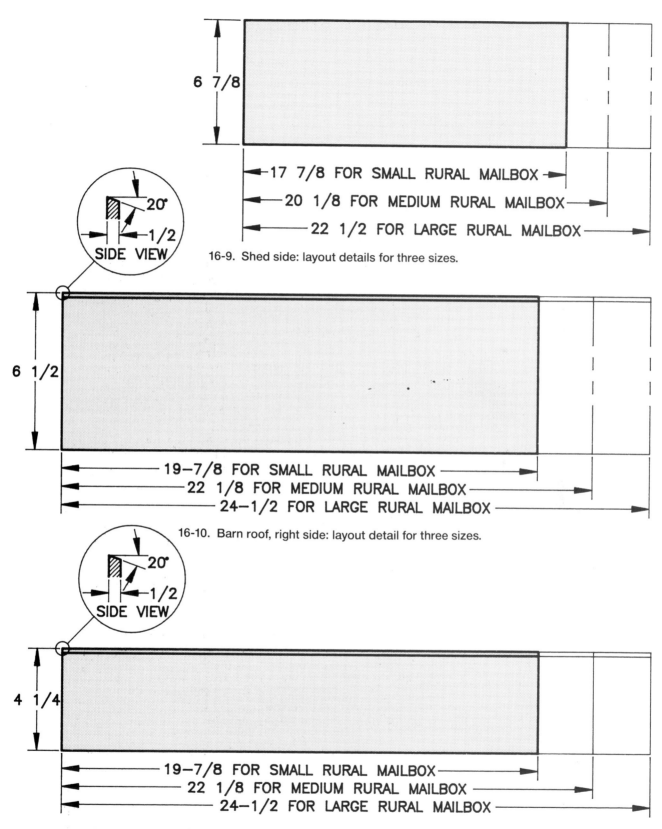

6 7/8

←— 17 7/8 FOR SMALL RURAL MAILBOX —→

←— 20 1/8 FOR MEDIUM RURAL MAILBOX —→

←— 22 1/2 FOR LARGE RURAL MAILBOX —→

16-9. Shed side: layout details for three sizes.

20°

1/2

SIDE VIEW

6 1/2

←— 19–7/8 FOR SMALL RURAL MAILBOX —→

←— 22 1/8 FOR MEDIUM RURAL MAILBOX —→

←— 24–1/2 FOR LARGE RURAL MAILBOX —→

16-10. Barn roof, right side: layout detail for three sizes.

20°

1/2

SIDE VIEW

4 1/4

←— 19–7/8 FOR SMALL RURAL MAILBOX —→

←— 22 1/8 FOR MEDIUM RURAL MAILBOX —→

←— 24–1/2 FOR LARGE RURAL MAILBOX —→

16-11. Barn roof, left side: layout detail for three sizes.

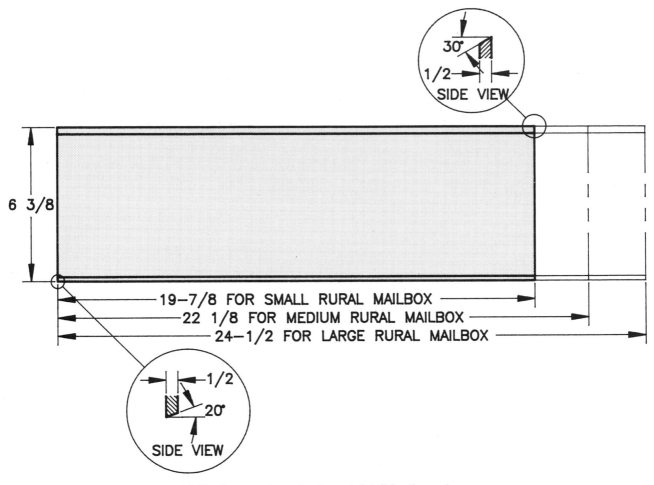

30°

1/2

SIDE VIEW

6 3/8

1/2

20°

SIDE VIEW

19−7/8 FOR SMALL RURAL MAILBOX

22 1/8 FOR MEDIUM RURAL MAILBOX

24−1/2 FOR LARGE RURAL MAILBOX

16-12. Barn roof, center: layout detail for three sizes.

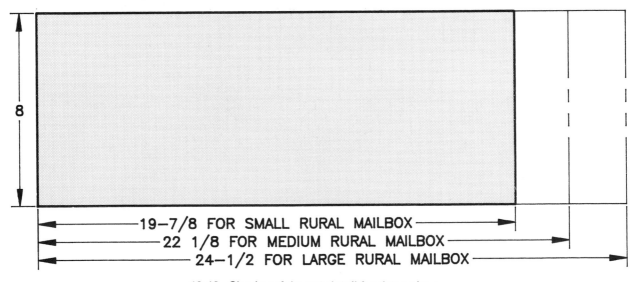

8

19−7/8 FOR SMALL RURAL MAILBOX

22 1/8 FOR MEDIUM RURAL MAILBOX

24−1/2 FOR LARGE RURAL MAILBOX

16-13. Shed roof: layout detail for three sizes.

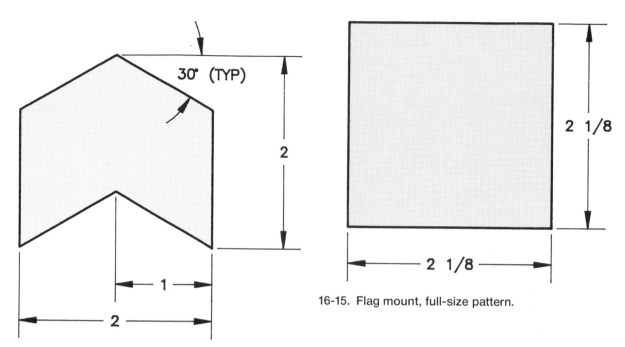

30° (TYP)

2

1

2

16-14. Cupola, full-size pattern.

2 1/8

2 1/8

16-15. Flag mount, full-size pattern.

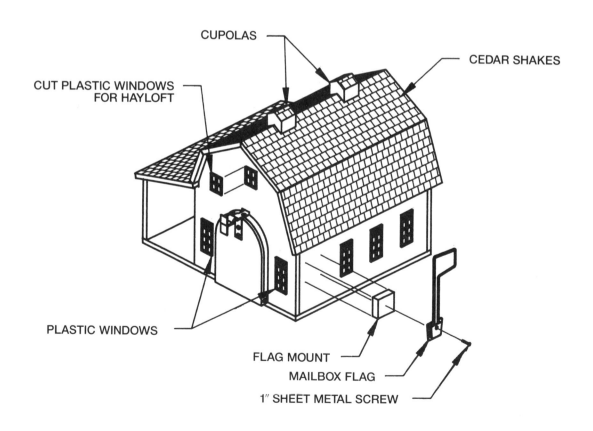

CUPOLAS

CEDAR SHAKES

CUT PLASTIC WINDOWS
FOR HAYLOFT

PLASTIC WINDOWS

FLAG MOUNT

MAILBOX FLAG

1″ SHEET METAL SCREW

16-16. Final assembly.

17
Fishing Boy

Bring back those lazy days of summer with this fishing boy mailbox symbolizing the carefree days of childhood. This is a wonderful conversation piece and a must for every angler.

This project is constructed primarily from 1½″ stock, which is cut, sanded, painted, and attached to a small mailbox. See the exploded assembly drawing.

Table 17-1 lists the materials required.

Cutting the Parts

Baseboard. Cut the baseboard to fit the recess under the mailbox. Attach it to the mailbox temporarily with several screws on each side.

Body and Legs. Transfer the body (17-2) and leg (17-4) patterns to 1½″ thick stock and cut out. Drill all holes. Attach the legs to the body with 2½″ × #8 screws driven from the rear. See 17-5.

The plastic eyes and black oval mouth are inserted into ¼″ holes drilled after the project has been painted. *Note:* Shank holes for the plastic eyes and black oval are not needed if you are going to paint the eye and mouth details on the wood.

Arms. Transfer the left (17-6) and right arm (17-7) patterns onto 1½″ thick stock and cut out. Drill all holes. Attach the arms to the body with 2½″ × #8 screws, as shown in 17-8.

Fishing Pole. A ⅜ × 16″ dowel is used to make the fishing pole (17-9). Mark the location of the holes to be drilled for mounting the screw eyes. One screw eye is located in the end of the dowel, and the others are evenly spaced along the dowel, between the hand and the end of the dowel (approximately every

2″). Drill 1/16″ pilot holes in the dowel and attach the screw eyes. Insert the dowel through the left arm and into the right arm, as shown in 17-9.

Fish, Hook, and Bobber. Cut two sunfish (17-11) from ½″ thick stock. Drill a ⅛″ diameter string hole through.

Drill a 3/16″ diameter hole through a 1½″ diameter solid wood ball (17-10) to make a bobber, or use a real plastic fishing bobber. Make a hook with worm (optional) from ¼″ thick plywood using the full-size pattern in 17-10.

Finishing

Finish-sand all parts. If there are voids in the center plies of the plywood, fill them with wood putty before sanding. Paint all wood pieces with two coats of latex primer followed by a finishing coat of exterior gloss or semi-gloss latex enamel. Paint color suggestions are given on the drawings for each individual part. Paint the eye and mouth details, or use a plastic mouth and plastic eyes, which are simply tapped into predrilled holes.

Final Assembly

Attach the fishing boy 4″ from the back of the mailbox. He can be attached facing either side. If he will face the flag side, it will be necessary to position him far enough from the flag so it operates freely. Also, the fish will have to be positioned elsewhere, for example, on the post.

Set the fishing boy on the mailbox and use a pencil to mark the location of the body and legs. Remove and drill three 11/64″ clearance holes in the mailbox. Reposition the boy and mark from the inside the ⅛″ pilot holes. Drill the holes. Insert one screw in the bottom of the body and one screw into the back of each leg. Use 1″ × #8 screws. All screws are driven from the inside of the mailbox.

The sunfish can be mounted directly to the side of the mailbox with ½″ sheet metal screws. Use a washer under the screw head, to prevent the tip of the screw from going through the fish (17-3). The fish can also be mounted directly to the mailbox post.

Attach the mailbox baseboard to your post. Re-attach the mailbox to the baseboard using ⅝″ × #6 screws driven through the lower lip.

Loop the string through the holes in the sunfish. Tuck the other end of the string under the body and cut off the excess length.

17-1. This nostalgic fishing-boy mailbox is symbolic of carefree country youngsters.

Table 17-1—List of Materials
(Dimensions are for a #1 or T1 rural mailbox)

Quantity	Part	Size of Material
1	Baseboard	*¾ × 6⅛ × 17½
1	Body	1½ × 5½ × 14⅜
2	Leg	1½ × 6½ × 8⅜
1	Right arm	1½ × 5½ × 7
1	Left arm	1½ × 3⅛ × 7⅞
2	Sunfish	½ × 3¼ × 5⅛
1	Wood ball (bobber)	1½ dia.
1	Hook	¼ × 1¾ × 3⅛
4	Sheet metal screw	½ × #8
3	Sheet metal screw	1 × #8
9	Sheet metal screw	⅝ × #6
8	Flat-head screw	2½ × #8
2	Plastic eye	1⅝ dia.
1	Black oval	¾ × 1⅛
4	Screw eye	¼ × ½ dia.
1	Dowel	3⁄16 dia. × 1
1	Dowel	⅜ dia. × 16
1	String	5 feet
1	Straw hat	6 inches
1	Brown mailbox	Size #1 or T1

Exterior enamel paint recommendations: yellow, red, light green, dark green, light blue, dark blue, white, light brown, brown, beige.

*Size of baseboard may vary, depending on the brand of mailbox.

Thread a second piece of string through the 25⁄64″ hole in the left arm, and insert the fishing pole through the same to anchor the string end. If the hole is too small, redrill it to 13⁄32″. Glue the end of the fishing pole into the hole of the right arm. Be sure the fishing pole is positioned with the screw eyes facing downward. Thread the string through the screw eyes and through the hole in the bobber. Secure the wood bobber to the string with glue and a 3⁄16 × 1″ dowel. Tie the hook to the end of the string and cut off the excess length.

Finally, glue the straw hat to the fishing boy's head.

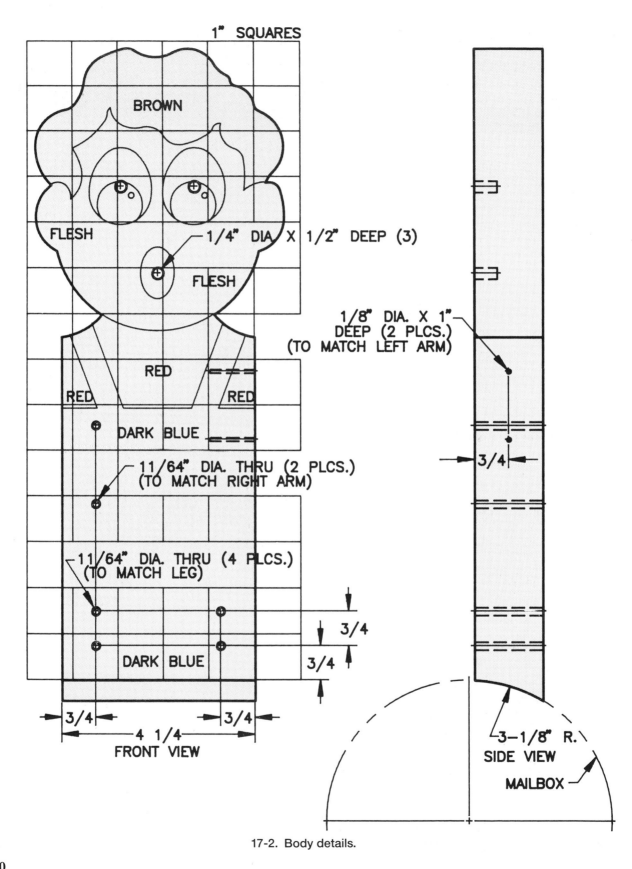

1" SQUARES

BROWN

FLESH

1/4" DIA X 1/2" DEEP (3)

FLESH

RED

RED RED

DARK BLUE

11/64" DIA. THRU (2 PLCS.)
(TO MATCH RIGHT ARM)

11/64" DIA. THRU (4 PLCS.)
(TO MATCH LEG)

DARK BLUE

3/4

3/4

3/4 3/4

4 1/4

FRONT VIEW

1/8" DIA. X 1"
DEEP (2 PLCS.)
(TO MATCH LEFT ARM)

3/4

3-1/8" R.
SIDE VIEW

MAILBOX

17-2. Body details.

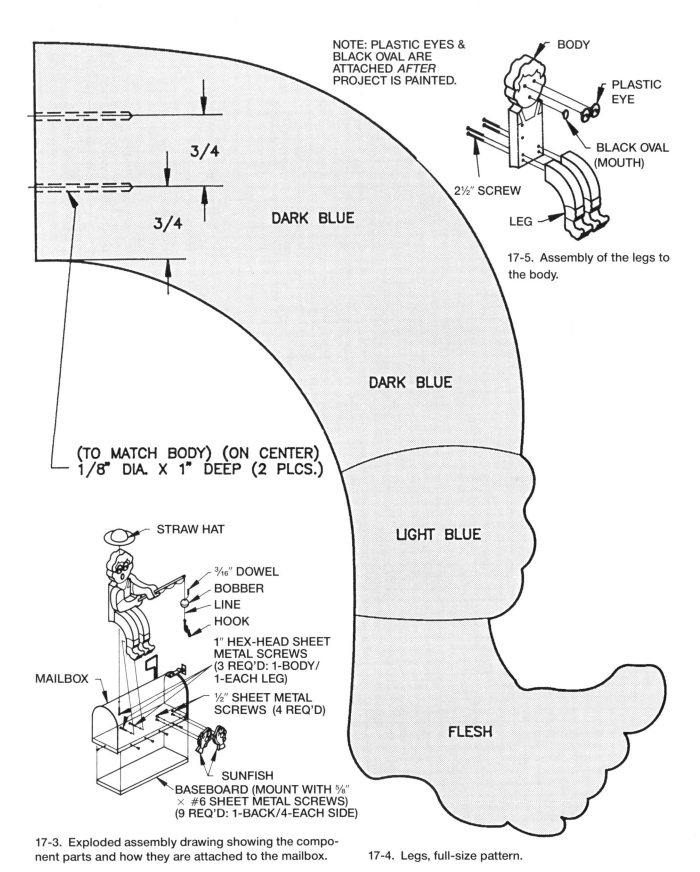

NOTE: PLASTIC EYES & BLACK OVAL ARE ATTACHED *AFTER* PROJECT IS PAINTED.

3/4

3/4

DARK BLUE

DARK BLUE

(TO MATCH BODY) (ON CENTER) 1/8" DIA. X 1" DEEP (2 PLCS.)

BODY

PLASTIC EYE

BLACK OVAL (MOUTH)

2½" SCREW

LEG

17-5. Assembly of the legs to the body.

LIGHT BLUE

STRAW HAT

³/₁₆" DOWEL
BOBBER
LINE
HOOK

1" HEX-HEAD SHEET METAL SCREWS (3 REQ'D: 1-BODY/ 1-EACH LEG)

½" SHEET METAL SCREWS (4 REQ'D)

MAILBOX

SUNFISH

BASEBOARD (MOUNT WITH ⅝" × #6 SHEET METAL SCREWS) (9 REQ'D: 1-BACK/4-EACH SIDE)

17-3. Exploded assembly drawing showing the component parts and how they are attached to the mailbox.

FLESH

17-4. Legs, full-size pattern.

151

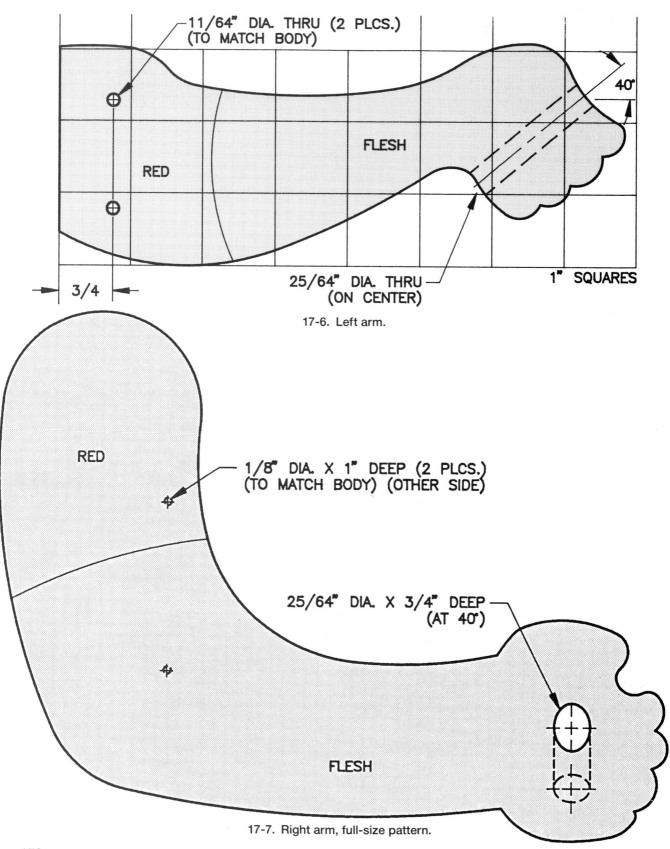

11/64" DIA. THRU (2 PLCS.)
(TO MATCH BODY)

FLESH

RED

40°

1" SQUARES

3/4

25/64" DIA. THRU
(ON CENTER)

17-6. Left arm.

RED

1/8" DIA. X 1" DEEP (2 PLCS.)
(TO MATCH BODY) (OTHER SIDE)

25/64" DIA. X 3/4" DEEP
(AT 40°)

FLESH

17-7. Right arm, full-size pattern.

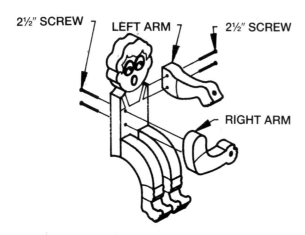

2½″ SCREW   LEFT ARM   2½″ SCREW

RIGHT ARM

17-8. Assembly of the arms to the body.

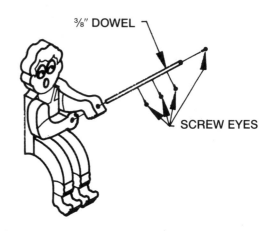

⅜″ DOWEL

SCREW EYES

17-9. The fishing pole dowel inserts into holes drilled in the arms.

13/64″ DIA. THRU

WHITE

RED

17-10. Hook and bobber, full-size patterns.

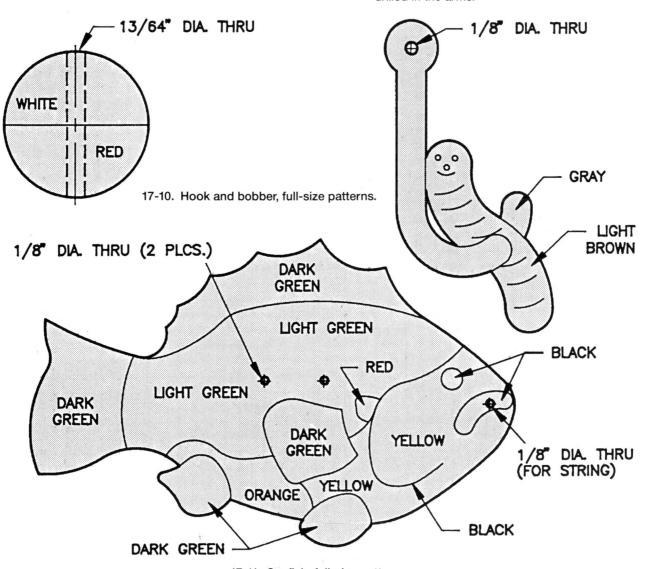

1/8″ DIA. THRU

GRAY

LIGHT BROWN

1/8″ DIA. THRU (2 PLCS.)

DARK GREEN

LIGHT GREEN

LIGHT GREEN

DARK GREEN

LIGHT GREEN

RED

BLACK

DARK GREEN

DARK GREEN

YELLOW

1/8″ DIA. THRU (FOR STRING)

ORANGE   YELLOW

DARK GREEN

BLACK

17-11. Sunfish, full-size pattern.

Appendix

Identification Numbers

Mailbox numbers can be added to the side or front of the project. We used precut wood letters on ours. Other choices would be to cut numbers from ¼″ plywood, purchase self-adhesive numbers, or paint the numbers on. U.S. postal regulations state only that the box number should be displayed. They do not have to be placed on the side of the vehicle like ours. Check #151.522 below for specifics.

United States Postal Regulations

Postal regulations do not restrict the decorating of mailboxes, provided the decorations do not interfere with normal guidelines, including the height the mailbox is mounted, the location of route or house numbers, and the ease of access to the raising and lowering of the flag.

The mailbox designs in this book do not affect the opening of the door or the placement of the mailbox flag—except possibly in the case of the church and barn, where the mailbox flag is mounted on the side of the structure rather than on the side of the mailbox. The only wood decorations mounted directly to the door of the mailbox are the feet of the goose, the tails of the ducks and horses, the cowcatcher on the locomotive, and the optional propeller on the triwing plane. These door attachments should not affect the opening of the door. Certainly, any of these decorations could be painted on the door if your postmaster or mail carrier objects for any reason. Also, you may want to paint these decorations if you add numbers to the door, as specified in Section 151.522, below.

All the projects in this book have been designed with applicable postal regulations in mind, and we believe they conform to all postal requirements. Our local postmaster could find no reason why any of these projects would not be acceptable to postmasters and mail carriers across the country.

However, it should be understood that postal regulations are subject to interpretation. Therefore, it is in your best interest to talk with your mail carrier personally about any mailbox modifications you are planning. When all is said and done, the mail carrier has the final say. We have found that taking a moment to talk to the mail carrier goes a long way. When you point out to your mail carrier the state of disrepair most mailboxes are in and your desire to take pride in your mailbox and keep it maintained, it is quite likely your carrier will be glad to give you a "thumbs up" on the project.

Listed below is important information from the 1992 "Domestic Mail Manual," issue #42, published by the U.S. Postal Service:

151.521 Custom-Built Curbside Mailboxes. Postmasters are authorized to approve curbside mailboxes constructed by individuals who, for aesthetic or other reasons, do not wish to use an approved manufactured box. The custom-built box must conform generally to the same requirements as approved manufactured boxes relative to the flag, size, strength, and quality of construction.

151.522 Painting and Identification. The Postal Service prefers that curbside mailboxes and posts or supports be painted white, although other colors may be used if desired. Where box numbers are used, they must be inscribed in contrasting color in neat letters and numerals not less than 1 inch high on the side of the box visible to the carrier's regular approach, or on the door if boxes are grouped. Where street names and house numbers have been assigned by local authorities, and the postmaster has authorized use of a street name and house numbers as a postal address, the house number must be shown on the box. If the box is located on a different street from the customer's residence, the street name and house number must be inscribed on the box. Placement of the owner's name on the box is optional. Advertising on boxes or supports is prohibited.

151.523 Posts and Supports. Posts or other supports for curbside mailboxes must be neat and of adequate strength and size. They may not be designed to represent effigies or caricatures which would tend to disparage or ridicule any person. The box may be attached to a fixed or movable arm.

151.524 Location. Curbside mailboxes must be placed so that they may be safely and conveniently served by carriers without leaving their conveyances, and must be located on the right-hand side of the road in the direction of travel of the carriers in all cases where traffic conditions are such that it would be dangerous for the carriers to drive to the left in order to reach the boxes, or where their doing so would constitute a violation of traffic laws and regulations. On new rural routes, all boxes must be located on the right side of the road in the direction of travel of the carrier. Boxes must be placed to conform with state laws and highway regulations. Carriers are subject to the same traffic laws and regulations as are other motorists. Customers must remove obstructions, including vehicles, trash cans, and snow, which make delivery difficult. Generally, customers should install boxes with the bottom of the box at a vertical height of between 3½ and 4 feet from the road surface. However, because of varying road and curb conditions and other factors, the Postal Service recommends that customers contact the postmaster or carrier before erecting or replacing their mailboxes and supports.

151.529 Newspaper Receptacles. A receptacle for the delivery of newspapers may be attached to the post of a curbside mailbox which is used by the Postal Service, provided: no part of the receptacle touches or is attached to or is supported by any part of the mailbox, interferes with the delivery of mail, obstructs the view of the flag, or presents a hazard to the carrier or his vehicle. The receptacle must not extend beyond the front of the box when the box door is closed. No advertising may be displayed on the outside of the receptacle, except the name of the publication.

Australian Postal Regulations

Mail services will normally be provided to a roadside mailbox or multi-purpose receptacle only where the road is trafficable in most weather conditions. The location of the mailbox/es is a point which is mutually convenient to the contractor, householder, and Regional/Divisional Manager. The mailbox/es should be positioned, wherever possible, in such a manner that the contractor does not have to alight from the delivery vehicle to effect delivery or to clear mail from the boxes. Delivery from a vehicle must be made without contravention of local and State traffic laws and regulations.

The size of the mailbox/receptacle, bearing in mind it may be a multi-purpose unit, but for mail purposes, should be at least 230mm wide by 330mm long and 160mm high, with a horizontal aperture size of at least 230mm wide and 30mm high, located 130mm from the base of the box. The mailbox should be of a solid construction, lockable, provide an adequate degree of protection from the weather, and be clearly identified with the roadside mailbox number of the owner's name and property name.

Canadian Postal Regulations

The projects in this book were designed for use with mailboxes manufactured in the U.S.A. Mailboxes of the same size are sold in Canada.

Rural mailboxes must be set 42" above the roadway on secure wooden posts, which cannot be wider than 6". Mailboxes must be on the outside edge of the shoulder of the road and must not obstruct other mailboxes. Rectangular mailboxes must be at least 7 × 7 × 18". Cylindrical ones, at least 10 × 10 × 18". Mailboxes must not be secured by a lock and should remain open while mail is delivered. They may have a lip or a flap to aid in opening. If a mailbox has a flag, it should be on the right-hand side when facing the mailbox. Rural mailboxes may not have anything on them that obstructs or potentially harms the delivery person.

Current Books by Patrick Spielman

Carving Wild Animals: Life-Size Wood Figures. Spielman and renowned woodcarver Bill Dehos show how to carve more than 20 magnificent creatures of the North American wild. A cougar, black bear, prairie dog, squirrel, raccoon, and fox are some of the life-size animals included. Step-by-step, photo-filled instructions and multiple-view patterns, plus tips on the use of tools, wood selection, finishing, and polishing, help bring each animal to life. Oversized. Over 300 photos. 16 pages in full color. 240 pages.

Classic Fretwork Scroll Saw Patterns. Spielman and colleague James Reidle provide over 140 imaginative patterns inspired by and derived from mid- to late-19th-century scroll-saw masters. This book covers nearly 30 categories of patterns and includes a brief review of scroll-saw techniques and how to work with patterns. The patterns include ornamental numbers and letters, beautiful birds, signs, wall pockets, silhouettes, a sleigh, jewelry boxes, toy furniture, and more. 192 pages.

Gluing & Clamping. A thorough, up-to-date examination of one of the most critical steps in woodworking. Spielman explores the features of every type of glue—from traditional animal-hide glues to the newest epoxies—the clamps and tools needed, the bonding properties of different wood species, safety tips, and all techniques from edge-to-edge and end-to-end gluing to applying plastic laminates. Also included is a glossary of terms. Over 500 illustrations. 256 pages.

Making Country-Rustic Wood Projects. Hundreds of photos, patterns, and detailed scaled drawings reveal construction methods, woodworking techniques, and Spielman's professional secrets for making indoor and outdoor furniture in the distinctly attractive Country-Rustic style. Covered are all aspects of furniture making from choosing the best wood for the job to texturing smooth boards. Among the dozens of projects are mailboxes, cabinets, shelves, coffee tables, weather vanes, doors, panelling, plant stands, and many other durable and economical pieces. 400 illustrations. 4 pages in full color. 164 pages.

Making Wood Bowls with a Router & Scroll Saw. Using scroll-saw rings, inlays, fretted edges, and much more, Spielman and master craftsman Carl Roehl have developed a completely new approach to creating decorative bowls. Over 200 illustrations. 8 pages in color. 168 pages.

Making Wood Decoys. A clear, step-by-step approach to the basics of decoy carving. This book is abundantly illustrated with close-up photos for designing, selecting, and obtaining woods; tools; feather detailing; painting; and finishing of decorative and working decoys. Six different professional decoy artists are featured. Photo gallery (4 pages in full color) along with numerous detailed plans for various popular decoys. 164 pages.

Making Wood Signs. Designing, selecting woods and tools, and every process through finishing clearly covered. Instructions for hand- and power-carving, routing, and sandblasting techniques for small to huge signs. Foolproof guides for professional letters and ornaments. Hundreds of photos (4 pages in full color). Lists sources for supplies and special tooling. 148 pages.

Original Scroll Saw Shelf Patterns. Patrick Spielman and Loren Raty provide over 50 original, full-size patterns for wall shelves, which may be copied and applied directly to wood. Photographs of finished shelves are included, as well as information on choosing woods, stack sawing, and finishing. 4 pages in color. 132 pages.

Realistic Decoys. Spielman and master carver Keith Bridenhagen reveal their successful techniques for carving, feather texturing, painting, and finishing wood decoys. Details you can't find elsewhere—anatomy, attitudes, markings, and the easy, step-by-step approach to perfect delicate procedures—make this book invaluable. Includes listings for contests, shows, and sources of tools and supplies. 274 close-up photos. 8 pages in color. 232 pages.

Router Basics. With over 200 close-up, step-by-step photos and drawings, this valuable overview will guide the new owner, as well as provide a spark to owners for whom the router isn't the tool they turn to most often. Covers all the basic router styles, along with how-it-works descriptions of all its major features. Includes sections on bits and accessories, as well as square-cutting and trimming, case and furniture routing, cutting circles and arcs, template and freehand routing, and using the router with a router table. 128 pages.

Router Handbook. With nearly 600 illustrations of every conceivable bit, attachment, jig, and fixture, plus every possible operation, this definitive guide has revolutionized router applications. It begins with safety and maintenance tips, then forges ahead into all aspects of dovetailing, freehanding, advanced duplication, and more. Details for over 50 projects are included. 224 pages.

Router Jigs & Techniques. A practical encyclopedia of information, covering the latest equipment to use with the router, it describes all the newest commercial routing machines, along with jigs, bits, and other aids and devices. The book not only provides invaluable tips on how to determine which router and bits to buy, it explains how to get the most out of the equipment once it is bought. Over 800 photos and illustrations. 383 pages.

Scroll Saw Basics. This overview features more than 275 illustrations covering basic techniques and accessories. Sections include types of saws, features, selection of blades, safety, and how to use patterns. Half a dozen patterns are included to help the scroll saw user get started. Basic cutting techniques are covered, including inside cuts, bevel cuts, stack-sawing, and others. 128 pages.

Scroll Saw Country Patterns. With 300 full-size patterns in 28 categories, this selection of projects covers an extraordinary range, with instructions

every step of the way. Projects include farm animals, people, birds, and butterflies, plus letter and key holders, coasters, switch plates, country hearts, and more. Directions for piercing, drilling, sanding, and finishing, as well as tips on using special tools. 4 pages in color. 196 pages.

Scroll Saw Fretwork Patterns. This companion book to *Scroll Saw Fretwork Techniques & Projects* features over 200 fabulous, full-size fretwork patterns. These patterns, drawn by James Reidle, include popular classic designs, plus an array of imaginative contemporary ones. Choose from a variety of numbers, signs, brackets, animals, miniatures, and silhouettes, and more. 256 pages.

Scroll Saw Fretwork Techniques & Projects. This companion book to *Scroll Saw Fretwork Patterns* offers a study in the historical development of fretwork, as well as the tools, techniques, materials, and project styles that have evolved over the past 130 years. Every intricate turn and cut is explained, with over 550 step-by-step photos and illustrations. Patterns for all 32 projects are shown in full color. The book also covers some modern scroll sawing machines as well as state-of-the-art fretwork and fine scroll-sawing techniques. 8 pages in color. 232 pages.

Scroll Saw Handbook. This companion volume to *Scroll Saw Pattern Book* covers the essentials of this versatile tool, including the basics (how scroll saws work, blades to use, etc.) and the advantages and disadvantages of the general types and specific brand-name models on the market. All cutting techniques are detailed, including compound and bevel sawing, making inlays, reliefs, and recesses, cutting metals and other nonwoods, and marquetry. There's even a section on transferring patterns to wood. Over 500 illustrations. 256 pages.

Scroll Saw Holiday Patterns. Patrick and Patricia Spielman provide over 100 full-size, shaded patterns for easy cutting, plus full-color photos of projects. This book will serve all holiday pleasures—all year long. Use these holiday patterns to create decorations, centerpieces, mailboxes, and diverse projects to keep or as gifts. Standard holidays, as well as the four seasons, birthdays, and anniversaries, are represented. 8 pages of color. 168 pages.

Scroll Saw Pattern Book. This companion book to *Scroll Saw Handbook* contains over 450 patterns for wall plaques, refrigerator magnets, candle holders, pegboards, jewelry, ornaments, shelves, brackets, picture frames, signboards, and many other projects. Beginning and experienced scroll saw users alike will find something to intrigue and challenge them. 256 pages.

Scroll Saw Puzzle Patterns. 80 full-size patterns for jigsaw puzzles, standup puzzles, and inlay puzzles. With meticulous attention to detail, Patrick and Patricia Spielman provide instructions and step-by-step photos, along with tips on tools and wood selection, for making dinosaurs, camels, hippopotami, alligators—even a family of elephants! Inlay puzzle patterns include basic shapes, numbers, an accurate piece-together map of the United States, and a host of other colorful educational and enjoyable games for children. 8 pages of color. 264 pages.

Scroll Saw Shelf Patterns. Spielman and master scroll saw designer Loren Raty offer full-size patterns for 44 different shelf styles. Designs include wall shelves, corner shelves, and multi-tiered shelves. The patterns work well with ¼-inch hardwood plywood or any solid wood. Over 150 illustrations. 4 pages in color. 132 pages.

Scroll Saw Silhouette Patterns. With over 120 designs, Spielman and James Reidle provide a diverse collection of intricate silhouette patterns. These range from Victorian themes to sports to cowboys. They also include mammals, birds, and nautical designs, as well as dragons, cars, and Christmas themes. Tips, hints, and advice are included along with detailed photos of finished works. 160 pages.

Sharpening Basics. This overview goes well beyond the "basics," to become a major up-to-date reference work featuring more than 300 detailed illustrations (mostly photos) explaining every facet of tool sharpening. Sections include bench-sharpening tools, sharpening machines, and safety. Chapters cover cleaning tools, and sharpening all sorts of tools, including chisels, plane blades (irons), hand knives, carving tools, turning tools, drill and boring tools, router and shaper tools,

jointer and planer knives, drivers and scrapers, and, of course, saws. 144 pages.

Spielman's Original Scroll Saw Patterns. 262 full-size patterns that don't appear elsewhere feature teddy bears, dinosaurs, sports figures, dancers, cowboy cutouts, Christmas ornaments, and dozens more. Fretwork patterns are included for a Viking ship, framed cutouts, wall-hangers, key-chain miniatures, jewelry, and much more. Hundreds of step-by-step photos and drawings show how to turn, repeat, and crop each design for thousands of variations. 4 pages of color. 228 pages.

Victorian Gingerbread: Patterns & Techniques. Authentic pattern designs (many full-size) cover the full range of indoor and outdoor detailing: brackets, corbels, shelves, grilles, spandrels, balusters, running trim, headers, valances, gable ornaments, screen doors, pickets, trellises, and much more. Also included are complete plans for Victorian mailboxes, house numbers, signs, and more. With clear instructions and helpful drawings by James Reidle, the book also provides tips for making gingerbread trim. 8 pages in color. 200 pages.

Victorian Scroll Saw Patterns. Intricate original designs plus classics from the 19th century are presented in full-size, shaded patterns. Instructions are provided with drawings and photos. Projects include alphabets and numbers, silhouettes and designs for shelves, frames, filigree baskets, plant holders, decorative boxes, picture frames, welcome signs, architectural ornaments, and much more. 192 pages.

Working Green Wood with PEG. Covers every process for making beautiful, inexpensive projects from green wood without cracking, splitting, or warping it. Hundreds of clear photos and drawings show every step from obtaining the raw wood through shaping, treating, and finishing PEG-treated projects. 175 unusual project ideas. Lists supply sources. 120 pages.

About the Authors

Patrick Spielman's love of wood began when, as a child, he transformed fruit crates into toys. Now this prolific and innovative woodworker is respected worldwide as a teacher and author.

His most famous contribution to the woodworking field has been his perfection of a method to season green wood with polyethylene glycol 1000 (PEG). He went on to invent, manufacture, and distribute the PEG-Thermovat chemical seasoning system.

During his many years as shop instructor in Wisconsin, Mr. Spielman published manuals, teaching guides, and more than 30 popular books, including *Modern Wood Technology*, a college text. He also wrote six educational series on wood technology, tool use, processing techniques, design, and wood-product planning.

Author of the best-selling *Router Handbook*, Mr. Spielman has served as editorial consultant to a professional magazine and as adviser and consultant to power-tool manufacturers. His products, techniques, and many books have been featured in numerous periodicals and on national television.

He and his wife, Patricia (Mrs. Pat), own and operate Spielmans Wood Works Gift Shop and Gallery and Spielmans Kid Works, both of which feature high-quality wood toys, furniture, and other trend-setting woodwork.

This pioneer of new ideas and inventor of countless jigs, fixtures, and designs used throughout the world is a unique combination of expert woodworker and brilliant teacher—all of which have endeared him to his many readers and to his publisher.

Paul Meisel's experience in woodworking and design is extensive. During his 10 years as an industrial arts instructor, Mr. Meisel realized the need for project plans that the beginning woodworker could manage. He began designing projects that excited interest in students, yet did not exceed their skill level.

Realizing the need for well-designed plans for the school as well as the home-hobbyist woodworker, he and his wife, Pat, set about creating a mail order company for the distribution of these plans. They took their unique concept one step further, by offering many hard-to-find specialty hardware parts. This company, Meisel Hardware Specialties, has become one of the nation's leading project plan and woodworking supply companies.

Mr. Meisel's company has published plans for over 1,000 woodworking projects, all of which feature Mr. Meisel's rigid criteria for simple, practical construction. He's dedicated to providing fresh ideas each year with a focus on clean, straightforward designs that create maximum impact, while using common sizes of lumber and simple painting and finishing techniques. He specifies materials and power tools that are readily available to the do-it-yourselfer. Full-size blueprints for all the plans—including the ones in this book—are available from his company.

He has received numerous awards for his woodworking projects. Many have appeared in books and magazines. In addition to his woodworking and design interests, Mr. Meisel is an accomplished writer. While pursuing his doctorate, he researched the area of educational gaming and published numerous games in the mid-1970s. Most of these games are still being marketed nationally. Based in part on his experience as a shop instructor, he published over 20 booklets in the area of technology education and has also written books on designing and creating board games, chemical safety, and measurement.

Index